# Praise for *How To Stand Up To Sexism*

*A punchy, practical guide providing
against workplace sexism. Exposes the
abuse and discrimination take — and
women might respond.*

**Kudsia Batool, He**

**T.**

*Universities would do well to hand out this book to all students at
freshers' week.*

**Anne Jenkin, Baroness Jenkin of Kennington, Life Peer
at the House of Lords, Co-founder & Co-chair of
Women2Win, Trustee at The Fawcett Society**

*Language is often a magnifying glass, the prism, through which we
experience gender inequality. How often have we heard sexist comments
and wished we had quick repartee to call it out? Well, this book can
help with just that. It provides examples of different responses: funny,
sarcastic, pointed, exasperated, factual — to a myriad of contexts. With
this book, language comes to the defence of gender equality. Language is
a tool to challenge everyday sexism — on the spot.*

**Helen Pankhurst, Women's Rights Activist**

*We all know the feeling — the French call it* l'esprit d'escalier
*— the perfect riposte only comes to you as you walk down the
stairs. Not anymore. With this brilliant handy guide, all women
will have at their fingertips the perfect response to any sexist
remark. Brava! This is a must for all the ladies in your life.*

**Eleanor Mills, founder of Noon.org.uk and former
Editorial Director of *The Sunday Times***

*An honest and practical guide to help women and men stamp out sexism and misogyny in society. Essential reading for all, young and old.*

**Sima Sthanakiya, The Curious Pixie
and digital content creator**

*Learning to challenge sexism and racism and all the other -isms that hold us back is some of the most important work we can do as humans. This is a brilliantly argued and super practical guide to empower women (and male allies) in a variety of situations. It will equip you with the tools and the talking points you need to stand up for yourself, set boundaries and shake tables. Thank you to Toni and BritMums for writing such a timely and necessary book.*

**Uju Asika, blogger and author of Bringing Up Race:
How to Raise a Kind Child in a Prejudiced World**

*An excellent and supremely practical guide to finding the right words to say out loud in those occasional moments when the idiocy of the world leaves you speechless.*

**Viv Groskop, author of How to Own the Room:
Women and the Art of Brilliant Speaking**

*With hundreds of responses to all the crap women have to deal with, there's something in this book for everyone! No more struggling to find the perfect retort for the everyday sexism women face. Just keep some of the brilliant examples in this book in the back of your head and wait, oh, a day maybe, before being given an opportunity to use them! What's not to love? A book to give you the confidence and vocal ammunition to respond to microaggressions and overt displays of sexism! This is a brilliant read for all women.*

**Tinuke Bernard, veteran blogger and creator
of the UK Black Influencers Directory**

*An incredibly useful book stuffed with insight, advice and anecdotes. Bravo, Toni and BritMums.*

**Helen McGinn, TV wine expert and international wine judge**

*As a father of boys and an LGBTQ public figure, I stand up for people who are discriminated against — and that includes women. This book has been a real eye-opener for me, not least because it so clearly explains all the forms of overt and covert sexism women face. With this book, I feel armed to be a better ally.*

**Jamie Beaglehole, lifestyle blogger at *Daddy & Dad* and LGBTQ campaigner**

*Men should stand up to the sexism that women face. This book will not only open men's eyes to the issues women frequently deal with, but it also shows how to be an ally, intervene and call out any poor behaviour they witness.*

**John Adams, award-winning dad blogger and podcaster at *Dad Blog UK***

*As someone who regularly finds herself sitting up in bed shouting, 'Aha — that's what I should have said!' hours, days, weeks and even months after a man has casually or intentionally thrown some sexism my way, this book is one I hope to see in pocket size (not that our clothes have pockets) so I can refer back to it regularly. A lighthearted attempt to help give us the tools to bravely challenge friends, colleagues, family members and catcallers in the street whilst making it clear the onus is on men to wake up and smell the misogyny.*

**Freya Papworth, advocate for ending violence against women and Co-chair of the Women's Equality Party Disability Caucus**

# How To Stand Up To Sexism

## Words for when enough is enough

Toni Summers Hargis
and
BritMums

First published in Great Britain by Springtime Books

ISBN: 978-1-8381746-4-4

The information in this book is designed to provide helpful information on the subjects discussed. However, this book does not constitute legal advice. Please refer to the resources in this book and/or seek independent professional legal advice if necessary.

Cover and internal pages designed by Cath Brew at www.drawntoastory.com

Dedicated to women everywhere.
Let's be heard!

# Acknowledgements

This book has had quite the journey, and throughout, we've been sustained and encouraged by the unanimous enthusiasm from everyone who heard about it. Thanks all; it meant a lot and reassured us that we were addressing an urgent but unmet need.

A book like this isn't complete without real-life stories, and many women stepped up to share theirs with us. We are truly grateful to you all, as some of your experiences make for uneasy reading. In order of appearance: Victoria Derbyshire, "Kate", Amy Sutton, Sima Sthanakiya, Uju Asika, Karen McLeod, Carol Smillie, Tinuke Bernard and Helen McGinn. Thanks also to the women who gave us permission to reproduce their tweets and material in the book: Jessica Huseman, Elena Cresci, Kim Goodwin, Clare Mackintosh and Susan Michie. Thank you, thank you!

From the moment we discussed the concept, our publisher Jo Parfitt has been a huge supporter. Jack Scott, Cath Brew and Paddy Hartnett, our team at Springtime Books, pulled out all the stops to get this book to market in record time. We appreciate you!

And finally, thank you to the friends and family who support women whenever we have to deal with situations like those outlined in this book, to women who have served as inspiration in responding to sexism with brio and grace, and to those who simply want to talk back to the inappropriate comments and actions, to make the world a better place for everyone. We hope this book gets us all closer to that goal.

# Contents

Hands On the Leg or Lower Part of the Body; Hugging;
Shoulder or Back Massages; Kissing (or attempting);
Non-verbal Attention; Groping, Assault and/or Rape

**66**

*Words have always been the tools, the weapons of feminists.*

Deborah Frances-White,
The Guilty Feminist

# Introduction

"I can't believe what's just happened!"

It's something all females have likely thought at one time or another when someone has said something inappropriate to them on the street or in a restaurant, touched them at work or on public transport. And often we find ourselves fuming but at a loss to parry the remarks – out of embarrassment, fear, concern for our jobs, not wanting to be rude or simply because we can't come up with the right thing to say in the moment.

Even during lockdown, the sexism has continued. Women working from home report being asked to dress more sexually or wear more makeup for Zoom meetings. Some find themselves more likely to be harassed on the street because there are fewer witnesses, and the tragic murder of 33-year-old Sarah Everard while walking home at 9:30 at night in London has produced an outpouring of anger and grief from women for whom harassment, unwelcome comments and threats are regular occurrences. Even women-centric businesses have seemed subject to harsher restrictions. Labour Member of Parliament Lucy Powell complained to *The Independent* (11 July 2020) of inherent sexism as pubs and barbers were allowed to open before beauty salons and nail bars. "Why is it that you can get your beard trimmed, but you can't get your eyebrows done?"

Good question.

We've had our share of annoying, embarrassing, unfair or dangerous sexism, and, like many women who've 'been there, done that', we know we can handle it so much better now. As mothers of young women and as 't-shirt wearers' who have researched, read about and written on sexism over the years, we want to share our insight with women who are finding their voices and looking for the right words.

In addition to our own 20/20 hindsight, we've collected advice and anecdotes from other women about their experiences of sexism, to highlight not only the prevalence but the variety of forms it takes. As you'll read, talking to other women and thinking about how you might deal with your situations helps you stand up to sexism and feel more confident while doing so.

## Why Do You Need This Book?

Women are still reporting sexism in disappointing numbers these days, despite the effects of the #MeToo movement. However – and this is the good news – the Fawcett Society, a UK charity campaigning for gender equality and women's rights, reported in 2018 that attitudes about what is acceptable have changed. In particular, attitudes are changing in the 18-34 age group. Respondents to their surveys who were aware of #MeToo were one and a half times more likely to say that their boundaries for acceptable behaviour had changed. Also in 2018, YouGov research reported that "Six in ten Britons (60%) say that the movement has made people more open to talking about sexual harassment. Just 2% think it has made us less open."[1]

This is something to celebrate!

There is a surfeit of books and reams of advice written about how to respond to sexism, and yet, there's still nothing truly practical to give women the personal tools to deal with sexism *as it's happening*. We see a lot of advice to "talk to the person in question", "make it clear that the behaviour is unwelcome" or "take the matter up with your boss/human resources", and it begs the question:

"YES, BUT HOW?"

Think about how often, when faced with harassment, discrimination or inappropriate physical contact, you've been too shocked or embarrassed to react at all. Instead, you freeze and fall silent, and are perhaps left feeling angry, humiliated, powerless or vulnerable. In short:

> *Women need actual words and phrases to help deal with the sexism they encounter every day.*

## What This Book Is… and What It Isn't

*How To Stand Up To Sexism: Words for when enough is enough* does not place the onus on women to *prevent* sexism. Let's face it, this is impossible. We cannot control how other people feel, speak or react. This book equips you and allows you to take back control. It's a reference tool and handy text to help you deal with snarky asides, on-the-edge comments and outright insults, firmly and appropriately. It's about giving you constructive ways to set boundaries and feel comfortable stating what you find unacceptable.

Most of all, we want *How To Stand Up To Sexism* to give you options; there is no 'should'. Every case of sexism is unique, and only you can decide. Is it safe to speak out? Is the person/comment/ situation even worth your attention? At work, will you be risking your job?

This book is not about policing men or educating them. Nor is it about demonising them. Men are not the enemy. However, at the same time, we believe women should not accept:

- the "boys will be boys" attitude
- that sexist comments are "just banter"
- that women should "put up with" sexist behaviour or
- that we should "stop being so sensitive" (often said by both men and women).

Sexism comes in many forms, ranging from seemingly harmless 'jokes' to threats of physical danger in the form of assault or rape. For many women, this sexism is coupled with other forms of discrimination; women of colour, trans women, women with any form of physical or mental health issues or different sexual orientations, for example, are even more likely to be victims.

*"Sexual harassment can target anyone but follows the contours of inequality — sex and gender, race and indigenous status, disability, immigration status, age and sexual orientation. Data shows the gendered characteristics of sexual harassment, that women and girls are targeted in significant numbers, that those with disabilities or who are LGBT+ or otherwise discriminated against (e.g. immigration status and race) are particularly selected for this discriminatory behaviour. Sexual harassment is not about random micro-aggressions: people are targeted for their membership of groups which are relatively less powerful than the aggressor."* [2]

While we might respond to various forms of sexism in different ways, we must remember that none of it is acceptable and all of it is damaging. Most offenders are relying on you not to say or do anything. Let's surprise them!

## How This Book Will Help You
Apart from giving you the actual words or phrases to use in situations where you're often tongue-tied, *How To Stand Up To Sexism* supports you when something doesn't feel right.

## Identifying boundaries
*How To Stand Up To Sexism* will help you identify your boundaries so that it's easier for you to recognise when they are crossed. To be able to tackle a problem, we first have to acknowledge that it exists, even when we're the person who is being negatively impacted.

# Introduction

As you read through the sections, you'll see just how many everyday occurrences are actually inappropriate and unacceptable. At present, much of it is so normalised that although you know you're not okay with it, it's hard to know if others would think the same, and that adds to any hesitation you may have.

Many women we've spoken to about sexism look back on their experiences and realise that their younger selves didn't even recognise how inappropriate or illegal the behaviour was. Journalist and television newscaster Victoria Derbyshire told us about her experience as a rookie and reflected on how she would handle things now:

> *"I discovered that my male co-presenter was being paid nearly three times what I was paid for doing the same job — co-presenting a speech radio breakfast show. It was true he had more radio experience than me, but I had more journalistic experience than him. I went to see the boss and explained that this wasn't right or fair (to my shame, all those years ago, I didn't know this was against the law or else I would have used that too). It was pretty painful trying to get my boss to see that there was something wrong and unequal. Eventually, over a period of months where I continued to go and see him and press my case, he gave me a number of pay rises which brought me up to around half what my co-presenter was earning. That's where I left it. <u>If it were now</u>, I'd pursue it until I had achieved equal pay. My advice to women who discover they're in a similar situation is not to be afraid to speak to your manager about it. And know that the law is on your side — you have a right to be paid the same as someone on a higher salary doing the same job as you."*

Being unaware of boundaries happens at a more personal level too. Here's Kate, a 29-year-old teacher speaking about her experience at age 22 with a 30-year-old colleague. Many of you will relate to her reflections, and we've underlined the main points:

> *"He was very attractive, and my colleagues and I used to joke about trying to see if we could chat to him at the pub on a Friday after work. It felt harmless, but without me fully realising at first, he clearly took a shine to me. It progressed to him sending me e-mails at work when he'd have seen me walking around (commenting on my outfits, how I looked, what he felt about me). I should have called him out on it at the time (or reported it), but I didn't because my naivety and lack of experience meant that I <u>didn't understand how not okay it all was</u>. It progressed, and he became furious when I didn't accept his advances. He told me he had fallen in love with me, and he used to insist on us going into empty classrooms to 'discuss' our situation. Again, I cannot understand how I <u>allowed it to happen</u>. I used to think that it was '<u>my fault</u>' that he was behaving like this; that somehow I'd '<u>led him on</u>' or '<u>been too friendly</u>' or 'just being me' was enough of a reason."*

## Forgiving yourself

As with Kate, many women beat themselves up for 'allowing' something to happen in the first place. In professional settings, where, like Victoria, we pride ourselves on being well-informed, we may feel annoyed or embarrassed at not knowing our rights. The most common scenario we hear is not knowing how to react at the time, then replaying the incident over and over.

Broadcast journalist Amy Sutton speaks for many women here:

> *"Even though I'm an extremely confident person, I don't feel*

*comfortable confronting someone in the immediate aftermath
of them saying something inappropriate to me – instead I dwell
on it for the rest of the day and then visualise every alternate
scenario of me actually sticking up for myself."*

Sima Sthanakiya, also known as award-winning travel influencer
The Curious Pixie, spent years working in TV production, which
she describes as "… an industry unfortunately still rife with
inequality and archaic ideas". She told us about an incident and a
reaction that are all too familiar.

*"I remember once being on a shoot and hauling some camera
equipment into a room, which I was perfectly capable of doing,
and a sound guy taking it off my hands, saying, 'We wouldn't
want you to break your pretty nails.' I wish now I was brave
enough to say something back, instead I just stood there a bit
gobsmacked as the rest of the crew smirked. I never put his name
forward for another location shoot again!"*

Regret about an incident or a comment can stay with us for
decades too. Dame Joan Bakewell, a veteran writer, broadcaster
and journalist, recently looked back on what was initially termed
a "joke" and sees it slightly differently now. In an interview with
Times Radio (20 September 2020), she discussed being referred
to as the "thinking man's crumpet" by fellow broadcaster and TV
personality Frank Muir back in the 1960s.

*"I thought it was just silly, his little joke… but it got picked
up a great deal. It hung around my neck for a long time and
perpetuated a sense that I was frivolous… It was a label I
could have done without."*

Dame Joan's experience is what's known as a microaggression,
or low-level sexism. Women are reporting that as blatant sexism

is being stamped out, they're experiencing more of this stuff. With microaggressions, sometimes the damage isn't immediately apparent. Demanding that women "put up with it" or "shake it off" seeks to keep us in our place and maintains the acceptability of women being treated disrespectfully.

## Speaking out with confidence

Uju Asika, an award-nominated blogger and author, looks back on one of her many experiences of sexism, with some words of wisdom:

> "When I was 19, I failed my first driving test. I put this down partly to the fact that my driving instructor was sexually harassing me. During our lessons, he would stare at me throughout, making me uncomfortable while I tried to do stuff like parallel parking. When I asked him to stop, he apologised but I would still catch him leering. Finally, one day he reached across and squeezed my thigh. I cancelled our lessons instantly and got a new instructor for the last couple of lessons. But by the time my test came around, my confidence was at a low. Unfortunately this was far from the first (or the worst) experience of sexism or harassment I faced growing up and into early adulthood.

> "Looking back on it, I wish I had done more than switch instructors. I wish I had reported him. But I was a teenager and he was a middle-aged man and I just wanted to forget the whole thing. It's an extremely vulnerable position to find yourself in as a young woman, being cooped up in a strange man's vehicle. If I had daughters, I would advise them to pick a reputable driving school (as opposed to an independent driving instructor) with a clear code of conduct. And if possible, to stick with a female instructor. I would also urge any woman who feels violated (whether verbally or physically) to raise their

*voice. If you can, do it in the moment. But even if it's years after the fact, tell your story. Even if the only person you tell is your therapist. You take back your power by speaking out."*

## How To Use This Book

We have divided this book into six different sections. *Section 2* contains general *Words* that fit a variety of situations. *Section 3* breaks things down into specific verbal issues and *Section 4* covers the physical stuff. Go to these sections when you're looking for ways to address sexism.

*Section 5* covers how sexists often react (otherwise known as 'the backlash') and what you can do in those situations. *Section 6* is devoted to showing others how they can help women facing sexism.

### Find your style

There are lots of phrases for many situations, so try them out, see which one sounds like you, or even practise them with a friend or a colleague if it's a work issue. We recommend saying them out loud so that you're more confident when dealing with the sexist, and you also build some muscle memory – your chosen responses will come to you more quickly. Different situations usually require different approaches; the pub isn't quite the same as the office, for example. You may go for humour in one scenario and something more serious in another.

There isn't a 'best' answer, just the best one *for you* at that time, to help you take control, and if relevant, to feel safer. This is particularly important if you find it challenging to be assertive, which, let's face it, runs counter to what's often expected of us.

### Your responses

As we've already said, this book answers the 'Yes, but how?' question. You know there's a problem, you've read all the advice about 'tackling it', and you still don't know what to say.

If you have a 'situation', there's a response in here for you. Even with a new problem, if you've glanced through the pages to deal with a previous one, chances are something will have stuck in your brain.

# 1

## Give Yourself A Talking To

Although we recommend a change of mindset, we're not advocating changing your behaviour, appearance or character and this book isn't tasking you with *avoiding* or *preventing* sexism. As you'll see, the mindset change is more to do with how you see yourself and what you have *the right* to do when standing up to sexism.

To get the most out of this book, you'll need to reframe things a little. Or, to quote the author Maya Angelou:

> *"You may not control all the events that happen to you, but you can decide not to be reduced by them."*

'Reduced' is a powerful word here because while a lot of sexism may seem trivial to others, it is typically designed to belittle you and make you feel inadequate and vulnerable over time. Many women report severe mental distress from their experiences and are 'reduced' to a shadow of their former selves. *How To Stand Up To Sexism* is here to help you claim the power rather than take on the burden.

> *"If people get in the habit of confronting, the fear and anxiety that is experienced when engaging in this deviant behavior should be reduced. Not all confrontations will go well, but some may go better than expected and reduce the likelihood of future biased behavior (Mallett & Wagner, 2011). If confrontation becomes commonplace, the defensiveness of those confronted and the stigma attached to those who confront should also be reduced."*[1]

Or as the sayings go, "Get comfortable with feeling uncomfortable" and "Fake it till you make it."

## Rules of Thumb

- You are not to blame for someone else's inappropriate behaviour.
- And they are not entitled to your compliance or your silence.
- If relevant, replace your need to be liked with a desire to be respected.
- Don't worry about appearing rude or offensive when someone is offending, insulting or scaring you. That person doesn't care about you, so that becomes your job. (And by the way, that's not telling you to *be* rude but just not to worry about 'how it might look'.)
- It's not the intent; it's the effect. Some people may not intend to offend or be inappropriate, so while you don't need to take the sledgehammer approach, it's still okay to address the problem.
- The result of not addressing sexism is that it usually continues. You are helping yourself in the short *and* long term by dealing with it as quickly as possible.
- Setting boundaries becomes easier with practice. As we said, fake being comfortable with doing it until you *are* comfortable with doing it.
- Speaking up about sexism is the first step towards change. Even if the person you think has behaved inappropriately disagrees, the culture will slowly change if other people start to agree.
- When a woman speaks up about sexism, other women see they are not alone. In turn, when they see you advocating for yourself, they might lend support.
- There is nothing snowflakey about calling out sexism. It takes a lot of strength to stop 'putting up with it'.

- Low-level sexism isn't 'nothing'. Just because things could be worse, doesn't mean you have to put up with the milder stuff. Putting up with it just means it won't go away.
- Standing up to sexism is not whining or playing the victim.
- Just because you can 'take it' doesn't mean you have to.
- Your aim is to shut down sexist behaviour, not to change someone's mind (even though that would be nice), so a debate is not necessary.

## Your Options

How you deal with sexism will depend on the specifics, which is why we're giving you so many options. Some situations call for a serious approach while elsewhere you can get away with humour. We recommend always being careful if you choose a more confrontational approach as studies have shown men often respond to perceived threats (to their status) with anger and aggression, which increases if this happens in front of other men.[2]

Your aim is to set boundaries and shut down sexist behaviour as opposed to debating the issue. Keep in mind that no matter how witty or withering your response is, if you phrase it as a question, it's an invitation to keep the debate going. If you have a question on your lips, try turning it into a statement with "It sounds like you're…" instead of "Are you saying that…?". A question is effective if it forces the guy to explain his offensive comment but should be used sparingly.

## To Ignore or Not To Ignore

… is worth pondering, as there are a few possible outcomes here. It's all about the context. Ignoring 'gateway' behaviour might encourage the offender to try again or take it a step further. Gateway behaviour, such as hugging, is often the stepping stone to more blatantly inappropriate behaviour. Ignoring crude conversation might encourage someone to step it up a notch to get your attention.

On the other hand, ignoring some things, particularly comments and catcalling, can indicate that it's not getting under your skin the way it was intended. For example, with interruptions, ignoring them is often a useful option to help you keep focussed and send the message that the interruption was not worth your time.

Ignoring comes in handy when the unwanted attention or comment comes from someone you otherwise respect or like. By ignoring, we mean not smiling at a 'compliment' you don't like, not saying "It's okay" when given a fake apology and not trying to make them feel more at ease than you are. In workplace situations, women often report not wanting to obliterate an otherwise good working relationship. We get that. It doesn't mean you have to put up with anything, but ignoring can be an excellent way to signal that you're not happy while also not reinforcing the bad behaviour in any way.

## Men Aren't the 'Baddies'

How To Stand Up To Sexism is not a battle cry. We know that there is often a lot at stake when challenging a situation or established practice, so there's no point in making things worse for yourself. And besides, most men are decent guys, even if they can be a little blinkered to all but the most blatant forms of sexism. Although we aim to help you stand up to sexism, there's nothing to say you can't call on some of your male friends and colleagues to support you.

## On Race, Ability and Other Differences

While we, the authors, are white women who have dealt with sexism for decades, we know that many surveys and statistics don't give the full picture. Many women are not only victims

4

of discrimination because of their sex, but because they fall into another protected category of the Equality Act 2010. These additional categories are: race, age, disability, gender reassignment, marriage and civil partnership, pregnancy and maternity, religion or belief. Studies on sex discrimination show much worse numbers for women who fall into more than one category.

We've written this book for women, and in general, about men, because that is our experience. However, anyone experiencing sexism can use these words and phrases; they even work in many bullying scenarios.

## It's Not You, It's Them

There will be many attempts to place blame at your feet when you speak up about sexism. In some instances blame might come from within as you second guess yourself, going back over the situation and berating yourself for what you didn't say. We've heard from a lot of women who've done that and we know the feeling. By all means, think of effective responses for the future, but don't beat yourself up for not coming up with them in the moment. Not coming up with the 'right words' at the time is perfectly natural and the reason we wrote this book.

Although the situations of sexism differ, offenders often throw out the same accusations or questions when challenged. Ploys such as deflection, gaslighting and playing the victim are all very common so we've listed them in the next sections, along with the *Words* you can use to stand up to them.

# 2

# General Tips On Taking A Stand

To avoid causing a fight or putting yourself in danger, talk about the problem or the conduct rather than about the person. Calling someone a name, while it might seem deserved, will usually make the other person shut down. You certainly don't have to go out of your way to make the other person feel better; just talk about the issues factually.

## Wait a Second

Sometimes we can be so shocked, angry or hurt by something, that we need to give ourselves a moment. That's fine, and in many cases, it will help you think more clearly and get the outcome you want.

## Be Firm

If you want to get the message across that something's offensive, inappropriate or rude, use those words. Tiptoeing around the issue allows the other person to debate it with you. Your goal is to stop whatever is bothering you.

## If At First You Don't Succeed…

Sometimes you need to say things more than once. When called out on sexism, some offenders just don't get it. Some refuse to even try, while others know exactly what they're doing and just keep pushing. In addition to her comments in the previous section, journalist and TV newscaster Victoria Derbyshire shared this story of persistence:

> *"When I first started presenting on the radio, having moved over from reporting, it was at the time when a younger woman*

*would be paired with an older man. Without fail, every day, the main 'heavyweight' political interview would inevitably be given by the producer to my male co-presenter. I worked very, very hard (and still do) to make sure my knowledge on any given political issue was in-depth and up-to-date so that I was able to start challenging (calmly) why my male co-presenter was always given those interviews, and could we please start sharing them more equally? It used to happen sometimes with sports interviews too – often they'd automatically go to the man I was sitting alongside in the studio. Why? I would ask. And gradually they too were split between us equally."*

## What To Avoid

As mentioned, this book discusses what to say when sexism is happening or has happened; it's not about prevention because we don't believe that's on women. As with any verbal situation though, certain words and phrases shut the situation down, while others can invite people to interrupt or talk over you. Unless you are genuinely mulling something over out loud, cutting out these phrases can be very effective:

- "Correct me if I'm wrong…"
- "This is just my opinion but…"
- "Sorry to butt in…"
- "I suppose it could be…"
- "Please." When you're standing up to sexism, you're not asking for a favour. Instead, say what you have to say and end with "Thanks" to imply that you expect it to be done.

Reacting with extreme emotion is often very natural, but it makes it easier for the other person to tell you to calm down or chill out. Given that you're reading this book to deal with a situation that has already arisen, you have a chance to practise what you want to say and deliver it with steely nerve instead of quivering anger. (Please note: that doesn't mean you should never show emotion, but many women report feeling frustrated with themselves for not being able to get their words out in these situations.)

Most importantly, when it comes to sexism, ignore demands to do the following, as they're all dismissing what you're saying and asking you to forget about it:

| | |
|---|---|
| Take the high road | Rise above it |
| Put up with it | Take one for the team |
| Smile | Get a sense of humour |
| Don't make a fuss | Chill out |

## Context Matters

We talk a lot about context in this book. It refers not only to the situation you find yourself in (Am I safe? Was that a blatant dig?) but to the person who's being sexist. Will they kick off? How do they usually respond to objections? Would they genuinely want to do things differently in the future? How you react to them will depend on what you know about them, which is why this book is full of options.

## What To Say in a Gazillion Situations

**The Words**

The tried and tested favourites:
- **Whatever you're trying to achieve here, you're failing.**
- **I don't want to hear that. (Let's talk about something else.)** Then move the conversation on. This states clearly that you want them to drop the subject.
- **That's not open for discussion.**
- Repeat their words back to them with an air of disbelief, then leave it hanging.
- If they're trying to stop you from discussing a situation: **So how would you prefer me to talk about this problem?**
- **I'm not** *making* **it a problem; it** *is* **a problem.**
- **Tell me why you think that's appropriate.**
- **Give me a minute to process that.**
- **Talk me through your thinking.**
- **Let's count the reasons why that's not okay.**
- **Did you mean to say that?**
- **I can't believe you even said that out loud.**
- **On what planet is your behaviour okay?**
- **Thanks for the insight.**
- **That's nice.**
- **OMG, you're** *so* **funny.**
- **I realise you're having a go at me to make yourself feel better, but it's still not okay.**
- **I'm just wondering what was going through your mind just before you said/did that?**

- **This is not a pie; if I ask for equal treatment as a female, it doesn't take anything away from men.**
- **This is not the 1950s/Dark Ages/etc.**
- **That hasn't been my experience.** (When someone makes a casual sexist statement such as, "Why do women always…?")
- **Interesting that it gives you so much pleasure to insult/belittle me.**
- If he's shouting at you: **I can't talk to you when you're so emotional.**
- **I notice you don't do/say that when there's anyone else around.**
- Taking all the fun out of things? **Fun for you, maybe.**
- If someone says what they're doing/saying is okay: **Fortunately, it's not your opinion that decides that; it's the law.**
- In answer to "He always does that": **He needs to evolve.**
- In answer to "Not again": **Yes, again. You're tired of hearing about it? Imagine living it.**
- **All I want is not to be spoken to/treated like this. It's not too much to ask for.**

At work:
- **Let's go and say that in front of HR, shall we?**
- **Just so you know, it's going to harm your career if you keep saying/doing this.**
- **It doesn't matter what you meant. And that's also the law, by the way.**
- **You are preventing me from doing my job.**
- **By the way, I'm taking notes.**

**66**

*I raise up my voice — not so that I can shout, but so that those without a voice can be heard...We cannot all succeed when half of us are held back.*

Malala Yousafzai, activist, Nobel Peace Prize winner

# 3

# Sexists – What They Say

As you know, sexism is often expressed through words said to you or about you. Dealing with unwanted attention and comments is one of the most common complaints from women. They can make us feel objectified, sexualised, demeaned and demoralised and can range from a 'joke' about appearance, to stories about the speaker's own sex life, and stalker-like behaviour.

One of the hardest things about coping with some comments is that they are frequently couched as compliments or defended as innocent remarks from someone "just trying to be nice". Other times, it's obvious they intend to belittle. When a senior doctor reported being called "a naughty girl" and "a little girl" just before going on stage to lead a conference for the British Medical Association, we can assume that the speaker meant to undermine her.[1]

The first thing to remember is that if a comment makes you feel uncomfortable, embarrassed, humiliated, insulted or scared, then it's not okay and you don't have to 'put up with it'.

Many harassers know that what they're doing or saying is inappropriate and they're testing you out – seeing what they can get away with. Some will back off immediately once you point out their offence, but unfortunately, some will push back out of embarrassment, guilt or anger. Try to remember that this is their emotion and not your fault.

*You're not 'making' anyone harass you in the first place, and you're not responsible for how they react to being told to cut it out.*

If you're worried about things being bad after addressing the problem, ask yourself if they could get any worse than they are. If you address the situation, you might feel bad for a while, but the original problem will no longer exist.

In work cases, the Equality Act 2010 usually covers sexism and sexual harassment and your employer must act when it happens. Experts advise that if you tell the offender his comments or behaviour are offensive or ask him to stop, you should keep a record in case the situation doesn't improve and you need to get a boss or HR involved. When it comes to discussing this problem in the future, documentation will not only help you remember but will allow you to remain professional and unemotional.

Concerning sexist comments, it's helpful to consider several things:

- The source – An unwelcome comment from an older person or someone from a different culture is not the same as the inappropriate dig by, say, a more senior male colleague. That can also be different from someone just starting out in business and learning what's appropriate. While out-of-bounds behaviour isn't excused, you can still tailor your response to the individual and the situation.
- The motivation – Are they trying to be friendly but doing it in an inept way, or are they intentionally trying to make you uncomfortable? If it's the inept-but-friendly person, you might be uncomfortable letting them know how you feel. Although we don't believe it's our job to educate men on appropriate, respectful behaviour, your response may help someone outgrow thoughtless behaviour.

Understanding and thinking about the root of these comments is not the same as empathising with those whose words are inappropriate or offensive to you.

## Being Called a Bitch

This is often the default when someone doesn't have a valid point to make. You can choose to ignore it, which is often advisable, or reply with these options.

### The Words

- I'm a bitch? Yes, that's <u>B</u>eing <u>I</u>n <u>T</u>otal <u>C</u>ontrol of Herself.
- Damn right.
- Is that the same as a man being assertive?
- Get used to it.
- I'll take that as a compliment since it's usually used for assertive and confident women.
- Smile and say, **Thank you.**
- Give 'em the Death Glare.
- That says more about your inability to deal with women than it says about me.
- Bitches get stuff done. (Quoting Tina Fey.)
- When a man gives his opinion, he's a man. When a woman gives her opinion, she's a bitch. (Quoting the late actress Bette Davis.)
- The fact that you have to resort to insults tells me you're out of anything rational to say.

# Catcalling

There are many definitions of catcalling, and we summarise it as:

*Unwanted, usually verbal, public attention of a
sexual nature, directed at you, which makes you feel
embarrassed, humiliated or scared.*

We've used the word catcalling as it's familiar, but this is harassment. Most women have experienced it. It can range from yells from across the road or through a car window to words said at close range by a guy who's following you down the street. Your response will depend on the circumstance and how safe you feel. Obviously, if you don't find the words offensive or scary, you needn't do anything.

In general, men don't seem to understand why catcalling is so deeply troubling to many women. In a tweet from Our Streets Now (4 October 2020), the organisation explained that PSH (Public Sexual Harassment) causes women to:

*"Change what we wear
Change how we feel about our body
Change the way we feel in public spaces
Affect and worsen our eating disorders.
It's never just a comment."*

Sadly, despite fewer people and cars on the streets during the UK 2020 pandemic lockdown, in a poll of over one thousand young women, Plan International UK found that one in five had still experienced street harassment and felt it was worse than before.[2]

Even if these guys know you wouldn't be interested, some can't resist a quick bit of street harassment anyway. Award-winning writer and performer Karen McLeod related a typical incident that happened to her and her partner:

> "*After years of having men shout things out at us, one day two years ago, a builder leant out of his van and shouted at us, 'I wouldn't shag you.' We were walking, probably arm in arm, towards the train station. The man probably felt threatened as often happens when they are faced with two women who wouldn't be remotely interested and are quite happy thank you!*
>
> "*[My wife] ran after the van, which was caught in traffic, and she was gone for ages, while I waited at the train station. She probably swore at them, and they went all sheepish as she stood by the side of them taking photos of their van.*"

If you're across the road from the hecklers, you can't say much, so ignoring, making a 'crazy' gesture or flipping them off is the usual response from women. If they're following you down the street, you should tailor your response to protect yourself. In these cases, sometimes ignoring the person ensures they keep following you, and at other times it'll make them give up.

If you choose to ignore, rather than saying something, that's okay. You don't owe harassers anything, including a response.

## The Words

Combing through the feedback from women on the Internet, most of us say nothing at the time, then wish we'd had the presence of mind to react differently. Don't beat yourself up about this, but perhaps have a few responses up your sleeve.

Joke about it:
- **As if...**
- **I'm betting this has never worked for you.**
- If they comment on a body part, even breasts: **Same to you.**
- **You're definitely punching (above your weight).**

Hold up a mirror:
- **Do you always compliment someone by making them feel shitty/scared/embarrassed?**
- **Why are you trying to humiliate me?**
- **If catcalling is okay, how come you never do it to women when they're with men?**
- **This is harassment.**
- **Not cool, dude.**

If it's really crude:
- **Don't talk to me like that.**
- **Does your wife/mother know you do this?**
- **Say that again so that everyone can hear.** (Look around to your audience.)

Embarrass them back (use with caution if they might get nasty):
- **As if...** (with different tone)

- **In your dreams, pal.**
- **Ugh, I think I need a shower.**

If they're following you:
- **What?**
- **Go away.**
- **Leave me alone.**
- **Stop following me.**

If you're worried for your safety, ask for help if you can:
- **Can I stand beside you until this guy goes away?**
- **I'm being followed. Will you walk with me?**

If it's safe, take out your phone and film him:
- **This is going on social media so everyone can see what a — you are.**
- **I'm going to the police with this if you don't leave me alone.**

**"**

*If you're effective as a woman, then they have to undermine you because that's a real threat.*

Nancy Pelosi, Speaker of the House.
CNN Television, 25 November 2018

## Comments Phrased As (Unwelcome) Compliments

This is a tricky one because many men would never think a compliment about appearance might be unwelcome, and some women wouldn't bat an eye. We're also definitely not saying all compliments are unwelcome. After all, how many people meet their life partners this way? The important thing is that if it makes you feel annoyed or uncomfortable or contributes to you not being taken seriously, it's not okay.

Writer Nadia Bokody nailed it in 2018 with her remark about compliments:

> "… behind every forced smile, fake laugh and eye roll, they [compliments] detonate a woman's worth in an already masculinised space."[3]

These comments can also be a form of what's called 'benevolent sexism', whereby men praise women for their 'feminine' skills and charms – a form of gender bias. Ironic, when you think that femininity often holds us back, and yet we're also supposed to be okay when someone wants to highlight it as a 'compliment'.

Rather depressing are undermining comments from older women like Edwina Currie (former Conservative MP) who declared on the BBC's *Woman's Hour* that she'd be delighted to be called "totty" (October 2017). You'll also hear women telling you to enjoy it as "it won't last forever". (Nothing like having your own feelings dismissed there, eh?) In June 2020, *Loose Women* co-host Carol McGiffin responded to the reports that catcalling had increased during lockdown with, "I just give up. It doesn't offend me at all. It wouldn't if it ever happened; chance would be a fine thing," and went on to suggest that anyone objecting to it was "overly offended".

Then there are male colleagues declaring that they love compliments from women; they completely miss the point that not only is this rarer than men remarking on a woman's appearance, but the typical balance of power usually means that it wouldn't belittle or embarrass them.

## The Words

- No words. Simply ignoring the comment can kill it and move everyone straight to the business at hand.
- Agree with the compliment. This is a tough one for many women, but cheekily agreeing with someone who's saying you look great, usually stops the commenter from saying any more and also indicates that you are confident enough not to need the boost from a male. **I know** or **Yup, I love this skirt/jacket** etc. deals with the comment and keeps things moving.
- The jokey **Aren't you going to comment on Ian's appearance too?** highlights the fact that the comment was gender-based and not welcome.

With more crude 'compliments' (about breasts, for example):
- **My body is not up for discussion.**
- **If you're trying to make me feel good, that kind of comment doesn't work.**
- **If you're trying to make me feel good, you're failing.**

At work:
- **I'm also good at my job** is the best response when someone is making a big deal about how great you look at work.
- Or: **Have you seen my marketing report too? It's a beauty!** It doesn't have to be delivered in a mean tone, but it reminds everyone in the room why you're there.
- **I'm also the one with the most experience here** is great to add if it's true.
- **What part of a professional working relationship calls for comments about my appearance?**

# Comments About Your Clothing

Some of the most distressing attention is when it's about what you're wearing. In many instances, we're supposed to take the comments as compliments, so the person who claims to be complimenting you will not like you rebuffing them. Some comments can be relatively harmless, but an accompanying leer or gesture can turn them into something harassing or offensive. Either way, you can speak up.

Tabloid journalist and television host Piers Morgan reminded Brits on 9 March 2021 that this particular brand of sexism is alive and well. Commenting on a co-host's choice of attire, Morgan claimed his "eyes were slightly distracted this morning", before demanding that Charlotte Hawkins stand up and display her short dress (and legs, presumably). Despite her downplaying his antics and suggesting that there were "more important matters" to address on morning television, Morgan continued with, "Am I complaining? No, I'm observing." British women took to social media to reassure themselves that it wasn't, in fact, the 1970s.

Your clothing can also come in for sexist criticism from others if you've been on the receiving end of harassment or worse. "Well, what do you expect, dressed like that?" is a phrase often bandied around when women are catcalled and is still brought up in cases of assault and rape.

## The Words

- **Why are we discussing my outfit?** can often end the conversation and make a point.
- **I wasn't asking for advice on how to dress** also conveys annoyance at the comment. A slightly jokier version is **Gee, thanks for the style advice.**
- A disbelieving **Wow** followed by a mild shake of the head, sends the message that the comment belongs in the Neanderthal Age. (Apologies to the Neanderthals.)
- **I find it weird/creepy/confusing that you choose to make so many comments about my clothing** will let him know that you're not at all flattered nor are you intimidated.
- **I'm going to pretend I didn't hear that** communicates your displeasure, but with some speakers it might just invite repetition of the original comment, so use with caution.
- Change the topic in a very noticeable way: **Wow, did anyone hear that rain last night?**
- Or simply answer any comment with, **Why are you telling me this?**
- **What I'm wearing does not give anyone permission to touch me.**
- "I can see your bra": **Well, stop looking at it.**

At work:
- **Say that again and you'll be looking for a new job** gets across how unfunny you find the comment and implies you'll take the matter further.
- **Fortunately, how I dress has no impact on how I do my job** keeps it clinical (and unemotional) and still puts the guy on notice that his comment was not appropriate.
- **I'm pretty sure I needed my previous experience/ degree more than my dress sense to get this job.**

25

## Comments About Your Physical Build

Except for cosmetic surgery, there's not a lot most of us can do about our physical traits. Height, arm length, foot size, etc., we're all stuck with it, which often makes comments more tiresome.

Here's author and writing teacher Aubrey Hirsch (@ aubreyhirsch) sharing her frustrations on Twitter in May 2020: "Are you even a woman in academia if your course evaluations don't give you feedback about your physical appearance?"

In some cases, observations about your height (if you're very tall, for example) might be thoughtless but not necessarily mean, and lashing out might not be warranted. For instance, in that case, the question "Wow, how tall are you?" might stem from inadequacy a shorter person might be feeling.

Comments about your bust size, bottom or any other part of your body that is commonly sexualised are generally not appropriate and certainly not at work.

Birmingham University Professor Heather Widdows launched an #everydaylookism campaign to help end body shaming, or 'lookism'. She invited people to share their stories of casual body shaming, and let's just say, it's pretty evident to us that men and women all need to work on that. Learn about the project on Twitter, Instagram and Facebook. Professor Widdows reminds us that:

> "Negative comments about people's bodies matter. It is not trivial; it is not 'just banter'. Comments about how we look can stay with us for a very long time. Body shaming is always people shaming. But we don't have to put up with it."

## The Words

Physical appearance 'feedback' can be met with varying degrees of tolerance on your part. Sometimes a long stare and silence is the best answer, as is a broad smile while tilting your head to the side to indicate that it's an old, tired comment. Other options include:

- **I was born this way.** (Extra points if you can Lady Gaga it.)
- **I like my ears/nose/forehead, thank you.**
- If you're feeling really cheesed off, try, **Wow, no one's ever said that before** or
- **Where are your manners?**
- Refer to the stickers at the EverydayLookism Insta account and quote a few.
- **Reminder: you can dislike someone's appearance and say nothing.**
- **Why are you discussing my appearance?**
- **Are you going to comment on Luke's appearance now?**
- **My body is not up for discussion.**

If it's a problem you've already addressed, we advise a firm warning:

- **I told you last week that your comments weren't okay, so I'm assuming we won't have a repetition today.**
- **I didn't make a fuss last time this happened, but *this* time I will.**
- **I've told you it's offensive to me and asked you to stop. Whether *you* think it's offensive or not doesn't come into it.**

**66**

*Each time a woman stands up for herself... she stands up for all women.*

Maya Angelou, author

Although it has become less acceptable to comment that someone is on the large side, smaller or thinner people still tend to be fair game. If someone says you're "tiny" and you don't think they're being kind, just say:

- **Would you be commenting if you thought I was overweight?**
- **Good things can come in small packages** and move on.
- Another one to try is: **You'll be patting me on the head next.**

Height comments, in general, can be dispatched with a swift:

- **Yes, I didn't have much say in what size I was gonna be.** (If you're really tall, check out a great blog called *More Than my Height*.[4]).

Comments about bust and bum are often best ignored, but these also work:

- **That is no way to speak to me.**
- **You'd better hope we don't start commenting on *your* body.**

At work:

- **I'd appreciate comments to be about my work, thanks.**
- **Those comments can get you fired.**
- **You might think it's funny but it's also against the law.**

## Condescending Language

This can either be fairly overt or so subtle it's difficult to complain about. The subtler forms – microaggressions – include referring to women as "girls", repeatedly telling women to smile and otherwise chipping away at someone's confidence or professionalism. Condescending behaviour (non-verbal language) can include being waved away by someone you're talking to, eye rolls when you speak, laughing or groaning at your comments or wrinkling a nose in disgust.

As with a lot of language, it all depends on the context. Being called "love" or "sweetheart" by some people can be completely harmless and inoffensive. However, while it's endearing when your grandfather calls you "love", if the word is used aggressively or condescendingly, to put you in your place or make you feel inferior, it's the opposite of respect. In between, there is the person whose culture (perhaps regional) or age means no harm is intended, but if you feel it's demeaning (for example, in the workplace), there's no reason you can't ask them to stop.

## The Words

If you're being called "love", "sweetheart", etc.:

- **It might be a generational thing/your thing, but I don't like being called darling** can be used with an older person. The "generational" option can be used as a barb if you're dealing with an older creep or lecherous colleague.
- **Do you call everyone 'sweetheart'?** is effective if you're in a mixed group, and only the women are being spoken to like this.
- If you don't care whether you offend the person, a simple **I'm not your sweetheart** will suffice.

General condescending language:

- **I'm trying to decide if you meant to insult me there** is another way of addressing the comment without laying into the offender.
- **Goodness, that's condescending** can be used if someone questions your knowledge about something that's relatively common knowledge.

## Customer Service

When Carol Smillie decided to buy her empty-nester dream car recently, the experience she recounted to us was a familiar one. The former actress and TV presenter had lots of questions, and the salesman had lots of responses – to Carol's husband. "I may as well not have been there. I was seething... I said, 'Helloooo, it's me who's asking about this car, not him.'" Her husband even tried redirecting the salesman back to Carol, with limited success. (It always helps when your man's on board; see *Section 6* for more on how they can step up.)

Needless to say, she bought the same model elsewhere – *because she could*!

The car-buying website Find & Finance listed the top things women hate about car buying, and second on the list was 'How can I help you, sir?' (9 January 2020). This happens so frequently because many women take a guy – any guy – with them to avoid being ripped off.

Tinuke Bernard, veteran blogger and creator of the *UK Black Influencers Directory,* remembers a similar incident with house-hunting:

> *"House-hunting is stressful enough at the best of times. Doing it single made it feel even harder as I had nobody to bounce my thoughts off of as I walked around. There was one house that I was on the fence about and in the end, it was the estate agent I had on the viewing that ended up being the tipping point to my decision not to go with it, rather than the home itself. After viewing the property, he flippantly remarked that I should get back to him with a decision after speaking to my husband. Not only was I not married, but seeing as I was viewing the house it seemed so offensive to assume I couldn't make a decision on it."*

We recommend always taking advantage of being in the driving seat (no pun intended) when you're making a purchase. Be it motors or mortgages, you can usually take your custom elsewhere if you're not happy. While you don't have to quote Julia Roberts in *Pretty Woman* ("You work on commission, right? Big mistake. Big. Huge."), there's no harm in letting salespeople know they're about to lose a sale.

**66**

*I do not wish women to have power over men; but over themselves.*

Mary Wollstonecraft, writer

## The Words

Although there are many more men selling cars than women, don't assume that all men will be sexist or that all women are going to focus on you. Even if you're buying something with your other half, salespeople should address both of you.

When they're addressing the male you brought along with you, start with one of these:

- **Actually, he won't be making this decision. It's just me.**
- **He won't be having a say in whether I buy this from you.**

If they persist in addressing the guy, remind them:

- **You're going to have to convince me if you want to close this sale.**
- **You can keep talking to him if you want to, but you won't sell anything that way.**
- Ask the male with you to walk away so that the salesperson has to address you.

If, like Toni, you've ever had workmen at the house who insist on your male partner being the decision-maker, try:

- **My husband knows less about this than I do; that's why we called you out.**
- **This is my decision to make, so there's no point in bringing him into it.**
- **He's not the slightest bit interested in this and trusts me to make the best decision.**

When they ask about "the husband" or "the man in your life":

- **I'm flying solo.**
- **I'm the decision-maker.**

# Hitting On You

Obviously, we're not saying no one can ever chat you up. Where would we all be without that? But what to do about the guys who just don't get the message that you're not interested or who ignore the signals you're giving off? Many women talk about not wanting to hurt a guy's feelings, and that's fair enough, but when you're made to feel guilty, or you feel undue pressure, it's time to put your foot down. Bear in mind though that many men will have had to muster up some courage to approach you or ask you out, so be kind if they're not being jerky.

### The 'boyfriend'

For some men, the only reason to back off is if they know you have a partner. If you're single, you're fair game. Annoyingly, what this means is they care more about offending someone they've never met (and whom they assume is a guy) than they do about respecting your wish to be left alone. Many women resort to the imaginary partner just to get rid of unwanted attention, and if it works for you, that's fine. (If he says, "Don't worry, he'll never find out," run!)

Women also resort to wearing a fake engagement or wedding ring to avoid unwanted attention at work or when socialising. Imaginary partners and fake rings though, mean that your own wishes aren't a good enough reason to say "Thanks, but no thanks". We can only really change this attitude by making it acceptable and normal to admit we're not interested.

### Giving out information

When it comes to giving out personal information, remind yourself (if you're not interested in them) that a complete stranger is asking you for this. You are not obliged to give them anything just because they're persistent. Even if they are showering you with compliments, there's no rule to say that in return you have to answer their questions, have a drink with them or do whatever it is they're asking.

## Men in power

Despite the best efforts of people like Dr Ann Olivarius, predatory professors remain a problem at many universities, and the problem still seems to be cloaked in secrecy. Dr Olivarius, an employment and discrimination lawyer, has represented students who were allegedly coerced into having sexual relationships with professors or supervisors. In December 2020, *The Sunday Times* reported that Oxford University was considering a university-wide ban on romantic and sexual contact between academics and students, recognising that such pressure was a misuse of the power balance in such relationships.

Although written from a fake professor's viewpoint, the website www.stopfacultypredators.org contains useful information for recognising when an academic might be grooming you for such treatment.

Working women worldwide recognise the problem of predatory bosses or clients, even if they haven't personally been a target. Again, these men use a power imbalance to pressure you into putting up with behaviour that is often clearly unwelcome and often harassment.

## The Words

- **Thanks, but I'm not interested right now.** (Don't get into a debate or a negotiation.)
- **I'm flattered, but I'm not looking for a relationship at the moment.**
- **I'm sure you're very nice, but I'm not interested.**
- **I'm out with my girlfriends tonight so thanks, but no thanks.**
- **Thanks, but I just see us as good friends.**
- Just keep repeating your one-liner. If persistence is his game, give it right back.

If he gets shirty:
- **You're not doing yourself any favours either.**
- **You're making me feel very uncomfortable.**
- **You're deliberately ignoring the fact that I'm showing no interest.**
- **If I were interested, there'd be no confusion here.**
- **I have a rule that I don't give out my contact information to strangers.**

In response to "I'm not like that":
- **I don't know you from Adam, though.**

If he's asking for your contact info:
- **I'm sorry, you're a complete stranger, so, no.**
- **Tell you what, give me your details instead.** (And write it in a notes section if you don't want it in your contacts list.)
- **The fact that I'm saying no means I'm not interested.**

Predatory professors:
- Try not to get into a debate about what they're asking you to do, even if they assure you "it's nothing".
- If asked out for a meal, suggest the college cafeteria.
- **Why am I blushing? Because you're making me uncomfortable.**
- **Blushing isn't usually a good sign with me.**
- **I'd rather talk about my project/essay.**
- **I just don't think it's a good idea.**
- **Okay, I know you've/we've been drinking, but you still can't do that.**
- Document everything.

Predatory bosses or clients:
- Very obviously redirect the conversation: **Okay, where were we?**
- **It's part of my job and my nature to treat everyone with respect, and I would like the same in return.**
- **We're not here to talk about me; let's get back to business.**
- **I'd prefer you commented on the product.**
- **Okay, I know you've/we've been drinking, but you still can't do that.**
- **Sorry but I don't mix business and social.**
- Document everything.

# Interrupting

Interruptions are a fact of life and a fact of conversation. Of course, lively debate and discussion often prompt interruptions – conversations flow around each other, bubble up, and occasionally overrun one another. But the dark side of interruptions is that they can be disrupting and diminishing.

As with 'mansplaining', verbal interruptions are often a power move that results in you not being heard. On the whole, when a man interrupts a woman, he expects her to give the floor to him. However, before taking your interrupter to task, consider a few things:

- Your role in the dynamic. It's worth asking yourself if you may be talking too much or for too long. If you tend to stray off-topic, or 'waffle', an interrupter might merely be trying to get things back on track.
- How to tell? Listen to what people say when they interrupt. Are they summing up and moving the discussion on to a conclusion or next step? If so, you might want to review your style. However, if they are restating what you said and adding their opinion or information that might be interesting but not to the point, using some of the *Words* below will help keep them in check.
- Also, be aware of the person's body language and facial expression. Toni remembers a friend who ignored visual clues (in retrospect) and asked a colleague not to interrupt her when the colleague was trying to tell her about a traumatic life event. This woman still agonises over ignoring her colleague in a time of need.
- What kind of interruption is it? Although some women have men present their ideas to make sure they're heard, it's

not always a good thing if men interrupt with 'supportive interruption'. It can happen because the guy in question doesn't think you will succeed in getting your point across. Often called the White Knight Syndrome, he comes dashing in with reinforcements and ends up undermining you.

- Bear in mind that many people aren't aware that they're interrupting, so although you absolutely should shut down most interruptions, a sledgehammer approach isn't always necessary.

Countless studies over the years have suggested that when it comes to interrupting, men do it more frequently than women, and they interrupt women more than they interrupt men.[5] However, the studies also show that women interrupt women more than they interrupt men. A study in the tech industry which looked at verbal interruptions, intended or not, found that women in very senior positions can be the biggest interrupters of all. This led the author to suggest:

> *"Women don't advance in their careers beyond a certain point without learning to interrupt, at least in this male-dominated tech setting."* [6]

**66**

*Above all, be the heroine in your life, not the victim.*

Nora Ephron, author

## The Words

- Don't make your statements sound like questions unless you're looking for confirmation or you're voicing doubt.
- Keep talking – watch any woman on TV who won't be interrupted, and she usually does it by simply continuing and not allowing the other person to chime in. Make sure your tone sounds confident.
- Raise your voice – at the risk of sounding 'shrill' (or any other words used to describe the female voice), raise your voice to the level of the interrupter and then just a touch louder.
- Raise the palm of your hand if you have to, or point a finger indicating that you'll give them the floor after you're done.
- Give them your 'being interrupted' look.
- Say the person's name a few times to get their attention. When they look at you, continue with your point.
- Interrupt the interrupter.
- Say **I'd like to finish** but don't say "please" or "sorry".
- If someone's trying to 'allow' the interruption by saying "I'm sorry to interrupt", pre-empt the interruption with:
  - **Great, I'll get back to you** or
  - **I'd like to finish my point, and then we can come back to you.**
  - If you're feeling exasperated: **And yet, you're interrupting.**

# Mansplaining

There's a reason why the word 'mansplaining' has such traction these days – it resonates!

The verb 'to mansplain' entered the Oxford English Dictionary for the first time in 2018 and is defined as:

> *"(of a man) to explain something needlessly, overbearingly, or condescendingly, especially to a woman, in a manner thought to reveal a patronising or chauvinistic attitude."*

Here are a few real-life experiences:

**Jessica Huseman** ✔
@JessicaHuseman ···

Replying to @brokeymcpoverty

.@brokeymcpoverty had a journalism student take over my lecture to explain to the class why the math I was doing was wrong. He was wrong.

1:24 PM · Mar 22, 2017 · Twitter for iPhone

Tweets reprinted with permission.

**Elena Cresci** ✔
@elenacresci ···

Replying to @brokeymcpoverty

the Welsh national anthem and the Welsh language (I am Welsh and speak it fluently, this guy was English)

12:30 PM · Mar 22, 2017 · Twitter Web Client

The woman who coined the phrase, Rebecca Solnit, describes mansplaining as:

> *"... the intersection between overconfidence and cluelessness..."* [7]

Not all men are guilty of mansplaining, obviously, and it is not merely a man explaining something to a woman. As author Laura Bates explained in 2016:

> *"... it arises when men are brought up in a world that teaches them that their knowledge and opinions are worth more than those of a far more qualified woman. It happens when some men act on these ingrained assumptions. And its impact, particularly in the workplace, can go far beyond the initial annoyance. The only way to stop it is to change the narrative that sets up male contributions as superior in the first place, not to 'train' women to deal with it later on."* [8]

To this, we would add that some men try to mansplain even when they *know* they haven't the faintest idea of their subject matter.

Mansplaining often happens when there is an imbalance of power (perceived or real). Women who appear to do it are usually in a superior position to you, perhaps at work, and like the men, are doing it because they think they can get away with it or because this is what they've seen being used by male colleagues to their advantage. You'll know when you encounter them, and the required responses are the same.

Consider the many explanations by men about the #MeToo issue. Unlike women, most men have not been the subject of gender-based harassment or worse, and yet many speak about it with absolute authority, even telling women who report abuse whether or not they have merit. Actor Matt Damon was famously taken to task for his comments on unwanted physical attention versus rape. In a December 2017 ABC television interview, Damon suggested that we look at inappropriate behaviour and worse on a spectrum, saying, "There's a difference between patting someone on the butt and rape or child molestation." Fortunately, actress Minnie Driver (also a former girlfriend of Damon's) took up the mantle in a subsequent interview, saying:

> "How about it's all f***ing wrong, and it's all bad, and until you start seeing it under one umbrella, it's not your job to compartmentalise or judge what is worse and what is not... The time is right for men just to listen and not have an opinion about it for once."

In July 2018 author and tech designer Kim Goodwin created this flowchart in response to repeated questions from male colleagues about what constitutes mansplaining. To quote a tweet from Ms Goodwin, "It's a tongue-in-cheek chart I spent 10 minutes on, not a doctoral dissertation." We think it does a great job and recommend you keep it handy for future reference.

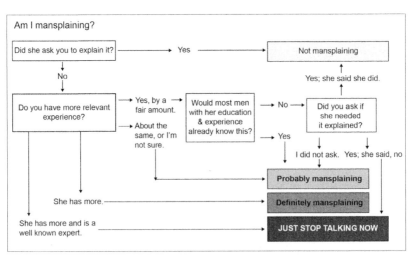

Chart reprinted with permission.

In a follow-up interview with BBC Worklife, Ms Goodwin explained:

> *"Mansplaining may seem like a trivial issue in isolation, but how we communicate tells other people how much or little they are valued. And in my experience, humans feel better, work more effectively and behave better when we feel valued ourselves."*

In a tweet in April 2019, author Laura Pearson (@LauraPAuthor) asked her followers for their examples of being mansplained to, kicking things off with her own: "Mine is when a man I met at a party told me my description of my actual job was wrong, and proceeded to explain why." Unsurprisingly, the responses to her tweet were hilarious and included a man telling the only Scot in the room that she was doing a reel incorrectly, cabin crew having aviation safety rules explained to them and a student being told by her boyfriend that she went to Newcastle University when she was actually attending Northumbria. Not only that, but he insisted on driving her to 'not her university' and almost made her late for her own graduation ceremony. (That response has now been deleted. We can only speculate on the fate of the boyfriend.)

**"**

*No one can make you feel inferior without your consent.*

Eleanor Roosevelt,
former US First Lady

## The Words

There are many ways to deal with mansplaining. Still, we don't recommend mentioning the word itself. This usually results in eye rolls, dramatic sighs of frustration, arm-flailing or accusations of sexism and 'womansplaining' – a term that has yet to catch on, incidentally.

- **Wow, for a second there it looked like you thought I didn't know what I was talking about** or … **you thought you knew more than me on the subject.**
- **Are you telling me this because you know a lot about this subject or because you have a *penis*?**
- **I see you've leapt to the assumption that I know nothing about this subject.**

If you're accused of 'womansplaining', assume a scholarly stance and explain:
- **Ah, there's a reason that word isn't used much. Mansplaining relies on the gendered assumption that men have more knowledge. 'Womansplaining' doesn't exist because the same assumption isn't made about us.**

At work:
- Faux surprise: **Oh, I'm sorry, I forgot to tell you my academic/professional background. This is old territory for me.**
- **I'm sure you don't mean to be rude, but I know quite a lot about this subject (which is why I've been asked to talk about it).**
- If he's explaining something he knows nothing about, ask a question. **Can you explain it for us in terms of X data available?** (He won't have the data.)

## Microaggressions

Low-level sexism, otherwise known as microaggressions, is sometimes the most difficult to deal with because you are told you're "making something out of nothing", "overreacting" or "always looking for something to be offended about". (Seriously. Do we need to go searching for sexism?)

As many women know, microaggressions take their toll and help preserve an environment of inequality, which can have more serious consequences. Or as author Laura Bates said in her 2016 Ted Talk on *Everyday Sexism*:

> *"The same ideas and attitudes about women that underlie those more "minor" incidents of sexism and harassment, that we're often told to brush off and not make a fuss about, are the same ideas and attitudes about women that underlie the more serious incidents of assault and rape."*

Disappointingly, it doesn't always come from men. In September 2020, Suella Braverman, Attorney General for England & Wales, and Advocate General for Northern Ireland, dealt a low blow to MP Ellie Reeves, labelling her "emotional" during a House of Commons debate. Her words – "I prefer to take a less emotional approach" – were unmistakably condescending and an age-old attempt to dismiss a woman because of her tone and delivery.

*Psychology Today* magazine confirms the damaging effect:

> *"Once your unconscious brain detects hostility in another person, it activates the amygdala — an area of the brain that processes fear — or other brain regions associated with a fight-or-flight response. This physiological change can make you feel anxious, fearful, worried, stressed out, or just ill at ease."*[9]

Because of the frequency of microaggressions, women often wonder whether it's 'worth' addressing them. Will it make someone angry or cost me a friendship? Do I have the energy? On the other hand, ignoring them could signal that you're okay with it or make you berate yourself later for letting it go.

There are so many examples it would take forever to list them, but we know them when we hear them. The phrase that stops you in your tracks, wondering if anyone else caught the meaning. The insinuation that you're somehow 'lesser' because you're a woman or you've just 'acted like a woman'. Trust your gut. Or as comedian Jo Brand said during Season 54 of *Have I Got News For You*:

> "It doesn't have to be high level for women to feel under siege [in somewhere like the House of Commons] and actually… if you're constantly being harassed, even in a small way, that builds up and that wears you down."

If only we could come up with a retort like bestselling author Clare Mackintosh. When fellow author Sarah Perry tweeted that she's often questioned about her husband's whereabouts when she's on a book tour, Clare replied that she's often asked where her children are. This is her go-to clap back:

**Clare Mackintosh 🐦 #HostageBook** ✅
@claremackint0sh                                        ···

I don't get asked this, but I am asked constantly who is looking after the children, and without fail I adopt a panicked expression and say: 'shit! ' knew I'd forgotten something'

10:57 AM · Apr 10, 2019 · Twitter for iPhone

Tweet reprinted with permission

## The Words

When deciding what to say, there are various approaches, depending on the person (and the context) and what you want to get out of any discussion. The person in question might not even realise how offensive or damaging the microaggression was, and can often react negatively to the explanation. Do you want them to understand why their words or actions are not okay, or do you just want them to stop? If you're going for discussion, that means you're not out to shame or blame, just to explain.

Waiting to address it is fine and might help you collect your thoughts, but you might also have to remind the other person of what they said:

- **Did you mean anything specific by saying X?** (Think of the "emotional" example.)
- **When you use the word X, it's very dismissive. (Did you know that?)** Focus on how you felt rather than arguing about what they meant.
- **Not sure if you realised, but it sounded like you were making fun of me just now.**

If you're not in the debating mood, don't let them tell you what you should be feeling:

- **Saying X is incredibly offensive to me, as I think you know.**
- **It's not really about what you intended; it's the impact it had.**
- **Telling me I'm being silly doesn't excuse what you said.**
- **I don't care if you think I'm overreacting. I think you were rude.**
- **That's a very sexist thing to say.**

Microaggressions are often deliberately passive-aggressive and vague. This vagueness allows the speaker to deny they 'meant' anything, so you have two options – completely ignore (with a sunny disposition) to show they don't affect you at all or show them you're no pushover:

- **Do you want to explain what you meant by X?** If they say "No" or "What?", reply with, **No, thought not.**
- **That's rather passive-aggressive.**

# Normalising

After the audio tape of then-presidential candidate Donald J. Trump was released in 2016, in which he bragged about grabbing women "by the pussy", the phrase "locker room talk" blew up. This, and perennial favourites like "boys will be boys" and "it's just banter" are used to whitewash and normalise inappropriate talk and behaviour by men, when it comes to women. They're the new "everyone does that here" and serve as yet another way of telling women to "lighten up".

Normalisation happens in every aspect of life and is not necessarily a problem; think about changes in the way we raise children (no more sending them up chimneys), what we do with our household rubbish and the fact that women's ankles are no longer a scandal. However, normalisation of all kinds of sexism becomes a problem for women because it means we report less of it; we report fewer incidents, such as workplace harassment, because really, was it that bad? Defences like Trump's locker room talk make sexist behaviour more acceptable and the pushback when we take a stand becomes louder and more vehement.

BritMums co-founder Susanna remembers an interaction on her street's lockdown WhatsApp group. The conversation started with a warning to beware that "Nottingham Knockers" (doorstep callers) were making their way along the road. The banter quickly turned into sexual 'locker room' talk. A reminder that this kind of innuendo was not appropriate for the group chat put a swift stop to it. "If I hadn't said anything, the messages and jokes would have kept pinging. Thankfully the group now steers away from talk about women's body parts and focuses on things like skilled worker recommendations or if anyone wants surplus Jerusalem artichokes."

Sadly, it's not just men; women do it too when they:

- Claim they can 'stand up for themselves'. That might be true but appearing to 'be okay' with sexist comments tells other women they should do the same, dismisses women who might need support, and ignores the permission 'putting up with it' gives men to continue being sexist. Especially if you're a public figure, there are broader repercussions of such an exchange – your 'blessing' makes it that much harder for other women to take a stand.

- Tell other women to 'toughen up'. Here they are sending the message that this is the world we live in (and we'd better just accommodate it). See the *Words* for our views on that. It also implies that they're somehow better than other women because they're 'tough' or 'resilient'. Perhaps instead of looking down on women who won't 'put up with it', tough women might want to show us how it's done and lend some support.

**66**

*Don't let anyone tell you you're weak because you're a woman.*

Mary Kom, Olympic boxer
and Indian Member of Parliament

## The Words

"He always does that" and "He doesn't mean anything by it":
- **That doesn't mean it's not inappropriate/illegal.**
- **I know it's easier to ignore it and let it continue, but I don't like it.**
- **Then he should stop.**

To "He only did it once":
- **Once was enough.**
- **What? So he gets credit for all the times he didn't do it?**
- **And if he gets away with it this time, he'll do it again.**
- **How do you know he's not doing it once to a lot of women?**

After a sexist joke:
- **Look around. Who do you see laughing?** (Only if it's just men, although women who laugh usually do so out of embarrassment.)
- **I'm sure you meant no offence, but that's offensive.**
- **It's *so* disrespectful to talk like that in front of me.**

"You need to relax/chill":
- **No, you need to stop talking like that.**

Being told to put up with it:
- **When you use the words 'put up with it', you're acknowledging that there's a problem.**
- **Just because you put up with it, doesn't mean it's right.**

## Offensive Language

Offensive language can be tricky as we all have different thresholds for what we consider crude or vulgar. However, ongoing offensive or crude language can be very wearing, especially when you know it's being done to get a reaction. The definition of sexual harassment includes offensive language, so you have a right to complain at work.

## The Words

We recommend you avoid name-calling where possible when dealing with inappropriate comments. Saying "You're a filthy pervert" might stop a few lewd comments, but it's just as likely to make someone angrier, so they retaliate. Sticking to the facts with a request to "Stop talking to me like that" gets your wishes across with less chance of a fight. Selective deafness is sometimes the best response to someone trying to needle you, but that's your choice, and no one else should be telling you to ignore it. However, we would avoid a reaction that shows the other person got under your skin – exactly what they were aiming for.

- Try no words at all. React as you would with a tiresome, naughty child and either frown, roll your eyes or raise your eyebrows.
- Try not to laugh at crude jokes, even if you're tempted to do so out of embarrassment.
- If you want to keep it light-hearted, use your best Mary Poppins voice and say:
  - **I think we need a swear box around here** or
  - **Now that's quite enough of that talk.**
- **Can you tone it down over there?** implies that you're not a prude, but the language has gone a bit too far. This is a good one in a 'lads' environment.
- To convey a slightly sterner tone, and put the swearer on notice:
  - **Guys, please.**
  - **That's not appropriate** or
  - **I find your language very offensive.** If at work, make sure the swearer hears you in case it becomes a repeat offence; then you can point out that you've complained before.

**66**

*It's about being alive and feisty and not sitting down and shutting up, even though people would like you to.*

Pink, musician

- Bringing attention to the remark can sometimes make the other person stop:
  - **Did you just say —?** If he says, "Yes, I did," nod knowingly and reply, **Yes, I thought you did.** This will give him the impression that you're taking mental notes, possibly for future action.
  - **Say that again** can be as innocent-sounding or as threatening as you want it to be.
- **Are you finished?** (eyebrow raised) lets the person know they're wasting their time trying to get a reaction.
- To the explanation that the offender "does that with everyone", don't accept this justification. It's still not okay.
  - **That doesn't matter; I still don't like it** makes your feelings known, as does
  - **Well, I don't speak for everyone, and I'm telling you I find it offensive.**
- If someone flatly denies having said something, perhaps because it was under his breath, just accept it and say, **Good, I thought you'd never say that.**

At work, it's not acceptable to be told it's just "banter". To this, you can simply reply:

- **It's inappropriate** and avoid arguing the definition of "banter".
- If this is a work situation and they persist in saying "It's just banter", refer them to the 2016 Trades Union Congress (TUC) report *Still Just a Bit of Banter?*
- Workplace swearing has been considered a form of harassment in legal cases, so a quick **It's a form of bullying and harassment** might make the offender see the light.

## Period-shaming

"You must be on your period" is the catch-all phrase designed to embarrass, belittle and negate us all in one. Like calling women "emotional" or "hysterical", our competence and intelligence is brought into question, this time merely because of a little thing called a uterus.

### The Words

- **Why? What difference would that make?**
- **Why do you need to know?**
- **What do you mean?** (These questions require the offender to explain precisely what he means. Make him spell it out.)
- **You must be period-shaming.**
- **Are you *trying* to humiliate me?**
- **Yep. How about you?**
- **Oooh, no. Embarrassed by women stuff.**
- **Well, at least I have an excuse for it. What's yours?**
- **I don't have to be menstruating to be in a bad mood.**
- Get technical: **Does menstruation embarrass you?**
- Or even more technical: **Throughout the menstrual cycle, due to oestrogen and progesterone levels, the brain changes. Our spatial skills improve at certain points, as does our perception and memory. Right now I'm particularly empathetic and communicative.**
- And here's an epic quote from @AlternateRowan on Twitter in response to "Don't mind her, she's on her period". **If I had to bleed to find you annoying, I'd be anaemic.**

## Playing the Woman Card

Probably one of the most difficult to respond to because it's so meaningless. When asked for examples, men who use this term can rarely clarify, but it implies that we're seeing sexism where there is none, blaming obstacles in the workplace on sexism rather than our shortcomings, or using our gender to get a leg up.

### The Words

- There is no 'woman card'; we get things done *despite* being women, not because we're women.
- The irony that a guy is suggesting I got something just because I'm female is not lost on me.
- What exactly does that mean? (Make him spell it out.)

At work:
- If the 'woman card' were a thing, we'd be dealing every day, and there'd be a lot more women in the big jobs.
- Oh, the woman card. You mean the one we play to get less pay for equal work?
- Are you suggesting that my promotion/pay rise was due to my gender? Possibly adding: Because if so, I'd be happy to walk down to HR with you to discuss that.
- You're saying that my achievements are entirely to do with my gender/sex/vagina and not my ability. And: Because if so, I'm sure HR would be happy to discuss that. Remember, you're not trying to change their mind necessarily, just shut down their line of attack.

## Putting You In Your Place

Although sexualising (below) seeks to do this, 'Putting you in your place' deserves specific mention because it's so common and often makes no attempt to disguise itself as anything else. References to domestic chores or barefoot and pregnant all seek to restore what the offender sees as the 'natural order' of things – men on top and women in their place.

Hillary Clinton faced this in her presidential run when men in her audiences shouted "Iron my shirts" while she spoke. Female celebrities (and authors like Clare Mackintosh) have had "Who's looking after your children?" thrown at them, especially when out 'after hours'. Examples you may recognise include calling you "sweetheart" in *that* voice and leering at you to remind you that you're nothing more than a body.

## The Words

- Sometimes the non-verbal eye roll is the best response to this malarkey.
- Or just ignore it. The aim is usually to provoke a response, any response.
- Let him know he's busted. **Is that you putting me in my place, is it Pete?**
- **Ah, the tried and tested put-down by the insecure male.**
- (Calling you "darling" etc.) **Oh, I'm not your darling.**
- **If you can't be respectful, then don't talk to me at all.**
- Or go for the burn: **Must be a generational thing.** Add a quizzical or sympathetic look.

At work:

- **I notice you don't talk to me like this when the boss is around.**

# Sexualising

When outperformed or challenged by a woman, some men see this as a threat to their masculinity and try to put the woman 'back in her place'. Sometimes this is with physical aggression, but more often it's verbally reducing the woman to her body parts. Occasionally men don't use words at all, but can still attempt to minimise the woman by, for example, staring at her cleavage or looking her up and down.

Sexualising though can be even more subtle when it sounds like harmless compliments. The example often given is when Facebook's Sheryl Sandberg first joined the board in a very male-dominated company. CEO Mark Zuckerberg's way to ease the tension was to comment on her beautiful skin, and joke that "Everyone should have a crush on Sheryl". Whether intentional or not, it emphasised to the men that Sandberg was foremost a pretty face rather than a formidable executive. As we said earlier, because these are 'compliments', women can be seen as too sensitive, ungrateful or man-hating if they voice an objection.

## REMINDER:

*From comments about "bedroom eyes" to hints about possible sexual encounters, sexualising is a power move and is not okay.*

Asking or telling working women to "look sexy" or "wear more makeup" is a form of sexualising women, and the COVID-19 lockdown did not change this dynamic. Employment law firm Slater and Gordon polled 2,000 women in July 2020 and reported that more than a third were asked to wear more makeup on Zoom calls. Almost as many were asked to dress in a sexier way. According to many bosses, it would "help win more business", "be pleasing to a client" or "look nicer for the team".

S&G lawyer Danielle Parsons says on their site:

> "It is categorically wrong for a manager or anyone in a position of power to suggest, even politely, for a woman to be more sexually appealing in the workplace. This is a powerful form of coercion which makes women feel as if they must adhere to the manager's request and be more visually pleasing to be successful at their job. This is demeaning to women.

> "Requests of this nature are discrimination and unlawful where male counterparts aren't treated in this way, or where such unwanted requests create a humiliating or degrading environment for women."

**66**

*I have always understood equality as not about demanding 'more' but rather being entitled to the same.*

Baroness Minouche Shafik,
Director, the London School of Economics

## The Words

"Show us yer —" Yes, sadly, this is still going on. Many of these phrases are at the front of the book, but we think they'll come in handy here too.

- **You first.**
- **Nah, they're not as big as yours.**

For many other unbelievably sexist comments:
- Say nothing and give a slight shake of the head.
- Repeat the phrase back to him, shaking your head and looking 'disappointed'.
- **Give me a minute to process that.**
- **Talk me through your thinking.**
- **Let's count the reasons why that's not okay.**
- **Did you mean to say that?**
- **I can't believe you even said that out loud.**
- **On what planet is your behaviour okay?**

At work:
- **Let's go and say that in front of HR, shall we?**

# Untitling (or Uncredentialing)

Although mainly work-related, this newly-named piece of sexism is popping up all over the place. Untitling happens when a woman isn't given the same professional respect in public as a man. Uncredentialing (a term proposed by Amy Diehl, PhD, and Leanne Dzubinski, PhD, in February 2021) is when a woman's academic credentials are omitted after her name. They are both microaggressions in that many people "can't see what all the fuss is about" – after all, isn't it petty to quibble about how a title is presented? Yet both these practices are extremely damaging to women.

As the President-elect Joe Biden and his wife prepared to move into the White House after the November 2020 US election, an opinion piece in *The Wall Street Journal* (11 December 2020) suggested that Dr Jill Biden should "drop the doc". Although Dr Biden earned a doctorate in education, the author was of the opinion that "'Dr Jill Biden' sounds and feels fraudulent, not to say a touch comic". So a woman using her official title based on her credentials is somehow comic or even misleading, according to the [male] writer – a stance defended by the paper's opinion editor who called it "a relatively minor issue".[10] Two days later Dr Biden tweeted the response:

> "Together we will build a world where the accomplishments of our daughters will be celebrated rather than diminished."

An omission, especially in comparison with men's credentials, has the same effect.

On 10 February 2020, Professor Claire Hopkins appeared on the BBC1 Breakfast show in her capacity as a surgeon. After the event, she tweeted a screenshot of the interview and commented: "Spot the difference... delighted to take part in an interview on BBC Breakfast this morning with my colleague. We are both Professors and Consultant ENT surgeons… why don't we get treated in the same way?" Professor Hopkins was referred to as plain old Claire Hopkins, while her male colleague was given his professorial title. Ironically, some suggested she should have addressed the issue privately, despite the error happening in a very public way. One male tweeter – who had Dr in his Twitter handle – suggested that she "Chill out".

She's not the only one this has happened to, which means it's not 'nothing'.

**Susan Michie**
@SusanMichie                                    ...

Just been on the radio with a male Dr. I am a female Prof. He was thanked as Dr X. I was thanked as Susan.
#EveryDaySexism

4:57 PM · Apr 23, 2020 · Twitter for iPhone

Tweet used with permission

Untitling women has multiple negative effects:

- It has the effect of diminishing a woman's accomplishments and expertise, especially when the woman is introduced/ featured/working alongside a man who's given his full title. Using a title for one person and not the other automatically makes people think that one is more credible and worth listening to.

- Addressing men in loftier tones than women perpetuates bias and stereotyping. Despite figures showing that more women than men are currently achieving postgraduate degrees, the impression remains that academia is a man's realm. A study in *Science* showed that girls as young as six believe brilliance is a male trait.[11]

- As with the *WSJ* writer's use of the word "fraudulent", there's a suspicion that accredited women somehow didn't work as hard, don't really deserve to use their title or are claiming to be more than they really are.

- It reinforces the idea that women should be 'modest', including when it comes to displaying their achievements. When Dr Fern Riddell tweeted in 2018 that she jolly well would use her title, it unleashed a debate as to whether that was arrogant, self-aggrandising or even earned. In response to some of the more pompous replies, Dr Riddell created the hashtag #ImmodestWomen and many women joined her in brazenly displaying their credentials! The hashtag resurfaced after the Dr Biden incident too.

- Untitling and uncredentialing can also be done in an effort to make women more 'approachable' or 'likeable'. Although we no longer (openly) tell women to hide their intelligence, studies have shown that when we look too clever, it doesn't do us any favours. Or as Natasha Quadlin, an Assistant Professor of Sociology at UCLA, found, "… women benefit from moderate achievement but *not* high achievement."[12]

As you'll see in the *Words* below, when women 'make a fuss' about this, we hear dozens of so-called reasons why it's no big deal. But it is. Credentials matter to women.

## Why women should use their professional titles

- They help us in already discriminatory workplaces. In other words, women have enough barriers at work; we need all the ammunition we can get, and that includes recognition of our credentials. It's often necessary to use titles and credentials to remind others that we're equal and up to the job, especially in predominantly male environments.

- Using a woman's professional title provides role models for other women and girls and provides visible, enduring reminders that women can do those jobs and that not every doctor or professor is an older, white-haired gentleman.
- They close the 'gender respect gap'. In her blog *Language: a Feminist Guide*, Professor Deborah Cameron uses this term and explains that "non-reciprocal usage (e.g. you call me 'Professor' but I call you 'Susie') suggests a status hierarchy in which one person must defer to the other".
- Dammit, these women have earned them. Or as Dr Biden told US talk show host Stephen Colbert, "One of the things I'm most proud of is my doctorate… I worked so hard for it."

## The Words

Although there are studies to prove that women are untitled or uncredentialed far more often than men (by both men and women), it's often more effective just to state your reasons for wanting to use your title.

Addressing the incident:
- **I'd like you to use my professional title, thank you.**
- **When I'm working, I go by Doctor and not Miss.**
- **Is there a reason I'm addressed as Ms. instead of Doctor?**
- **I don't mind you using my first name, as long as you do it for everyone.**
- **I'm here in my professional capacity and addressing me as Professor lets people know I'm an expert.**
- **It's a matter of respect for me that we're all addressed in the same way.**

"It's just a title":
- **Fine, then don't use it for anyone.**
- **Then why bother using it for him?**
- **And yet you/they used it for the man.**
- **If you introduce me as Sue and him as Dr Smith, who are they going to listen to?**
- **There are lots of (young) women out there and it's important they see the possibility of someday becoming a doctor.**

"It shouldn't be about the title; it's what you say/do that's important":
- All of the above *Words*.

- **It's hard enough to get credit for my work; my title just helps with that.**
- **In a perfect world that would be true, but the workplace isn't perfect for women.**

Telling you that you shouldn't embarrass anyone by calling it out:
- **I'm offended by his omission. It's not my job to ignore that just to spare his feelings.**
- **If I don't say anything, it will just continue.**

"You should have addressed it privately":
- **When we do that, nothing ever changes.**
- **And yet I was humiliated publicly.**
- **I did that the last time and look where we are.**

If 'ego' is even hinted at:
- **I worked very hard for this qualification and it's relevant to my work. I want people to know my level of expertise.**
- **It's not pretentious, it's professional.**
- **Have you ever seen a man accused of being arrogant for using his title at work?**
- **As a woman, I have to work hard enough to be heard in my profession. Using my title has nothing to do with ego and everything to do with the need to be taken seriously.**

# 4

# Sexists – What They Do

In addition to the many words and phrases sexists use to belittle or scare women, they sometimes resort to the physical.

## The Basics

What is sexual assault? The Sexual Offences Act 2003 (England & Wales) says:

> *"Sexual assault is when a person is coerced or physically forced to engage against their will, or when a person, male or female, touches another person sexually without their consent. Touching can be done with any part of the body or with an object."*

The Act lists the elements of the offence of sexual assault as:

- *A person (A) intentionally touches another person.*
- *The touching is sexual.*
- *The person being touched (B) does not consent to the touching, and the toucher (A) does not reasonably believe that B consents.*
- *Whether a belief is reasonable is to be determined having regard to all the circumstances, including any steps A has taken to ascertain whether B consents.*

This might seem to leave a lot of leeway in interpretation as to whether the toucher believes the other person consents – or possibly 'doesn't mind'. However, according to the definition, groping, grabbing, and fondling could be included, no matter who calls it 'harmless fun'.

The CPS (Crown Prosecution Service) guidelines further state that:

> "Touching is widely defined and includes touching another person with any part of the body, or with anything else. Touching can be through clothing ... the Court of Appeal held that the touching of an individual's clothing was sufficient to amount to 'touching'."[1]

(In Scotland, the Sexual Offences Act 2009 applies, and in Northern Ireland, the Sexual Offences Order 2008.)

What is sexual harassment? Citizens Advice describe sexual harassment as:

> "... unwanted behaviour of a sexual nature which:
> * violates your dignity
> * makes you feel intimidated, degraded or humiliated
> * creates a hostile or offensive environment
>
> You don't need to have previously objected to someone's behaviour for it to be considered unwanted."

'Behaviour' includes comments, looks, leers, physical acts, e-mails, pictures/posters of a sexual nature and promises of a reward for sexual favours.

Moves like grabbing a breast or a buttock usually fall under these categories, but what about the 'milder' stuff? While it's not all sexual assault or even harassment, if it's only done to women, it's sexism, and if it makes you feel uncomfortable, it has to stop. Since many of us don't like being touched by random people, whether it's sexual or not, we'll include it all under this umbrella because, as usual, women are expected not to 'make a fuss'.

You will often hear that the person touching you didn't realise they were making you feel uncomfortable. You can't get inside their head to argue the point, and that's not your goal – your focus is on ending the situation. Addressing the problem also ensures that you've clearly communicated your displeasure to the problem person.

This is what Victim Support has to say about sexual assault:

> *"If someone intentionally grabs or touches you in a sexual way that you don't like, or you're forced to kiss someone or do something else sexual against your will, that's sexual assault. This includes sexual touching of any part of someone's body, and it makes no difference whether you're wearing clothes or not. Anyone can be sexually assaulted and both men and women can commit sexual assault."*

## "He Just Had Too Much To Drink"

Let's get one thing straight: if alcohol were the cause of sexual harassment or assault, more men would be doing it to more women. Come to that, more women would be doing it to more men too! Most men seem to be able to behave appropriately even when sloshed (or even when the woman's sloshed), so the defence of having had too much to drink falls flat. The law doesn't look kindly on this excuse from an offender. If he's too drunk to even think about consent, can't remember or was mistaken in the belief that you gave consent, it's usually not good enough. The involvement of alcohol also doesn't mean that it didn't happen or that it should be swept under the carpet.

Sadly, the amount of alcohol female victims consume still leads to the idea that we somehow contributed to the offence – "What do you expect when you get so drunk?" A study by Dr Heather Flowe from the University of Birmingham found that the victims themselves often share this 'blame'.

*"It's concerning that women in the study were more likely to blame the hypothetical rape on their behaviour and character if they believed that they had consumed alcohol... Even more concerning is that the effects of alcohol on rape reporting in the real world might be even stronger than that found in the present research, given the intense levels of scrutiny that survivors are under in real-world cases."*[2]

We believe this is wildly out of line. If women are advised not to consume too much alcohol, the same should be said to men who might rely on that defence, since their inebriation won't protect them if accused.

## Consent

We hear this word a lot these days, and it's worth keeping it front and centre in your head if someone is touching you and you don't want them to.

What is consent? According to Section 74 of the Sexual Offences Act 2003:

*"... a person consents if he agrees by choice, and has the freedom and capacity to make that choice."*

Further:

*"Consent to sexual activity may be given to one sort of sexual activity but not another, e.g. vaginal but not anal sex or penetration with conditions, such as wearing a condom. Consent can be withdrawn at any time during sexual activity and each time activity occurs."*

Not only do you have to consent, but you have to be *able* to consent. Know that sometimes consent is given because the victim feels there is no alternative – she'll lose her job, be hurt, won't be able to leave the area, or things will turn otherwise nasty due to saying no. That is not true consent.

UN Women (the United Nations entity for gender equality and women's empowerment) specifically uses the word 'unwelcome' rather than 'consent'. It lists the following as not being 'consent':

Silence
A forced "yes"
"Maybe"
Unconscious
Drunk
Past consent (meaning you can change your mind)
A mini skirt
Flirting

## Intent
In some of the situations below, there's often some question about the intent behind the act, so we would encourage you to assume the best where you can and proceed from there. To 'assume the best' does not mean 'Let me figure out where I went wrong'.

> *For those in the back of the room:*
> *you did not cause it to happen.*

'Assuming the best' means considering whether the person is trying to humiliate or belittle you, versus whether they're just out of touch with what's culturally appropriate. The often touted "Oh he's like that with everyone" doesn't cut the mustard though. Fortunately, COVID-19 and other germ-related concerns give you a lot of cover when attempting to distance yourself from others physically.

## 'Accidental' Touching

Many of us know the guy who needs to 'squeeze past' or the one who always seems to stand just a little too close. Not okay. In our experience, these creeps usually know precisely what they're doing and rely on the fact that it could, at a stretch, look innocent. They usually flatly deny whatever you accuse them of, as well as then trying to make you look like the bad person – classic gaslighting. Don't accept it.

## The Words

As he approaches:
- Move so that you give him a wide berth, as well as sending a message.
- **Let me move out of your way; you always seem to have *such* a problem getting past.**
- **Don't tell me; you're going to 'squeeze through' again, aren't you?**

After it's happened:
- **Why don't you just walk around the other way? It'd be so much easier.**
- **There's no need to touch me.**
- **Next time you do that, do it without touching me.**

# Hands On the Upper Body

Bear in mind we're talking about people you're not in a relationship with or situations where you don't give consent.

### Hand on arm or shoulder
Men and women, young and old, do this; it's not always sexual in nature, and if it lasts less than about three seconds, most people will find this okay. In some cultures, people of both sexes hold each other's hands while talking and would have no ill intent. These people might be shocked to know they were creeping you out, so we advise assessing the situation and responding accordingly. If you're not a touchy-feely person, it's okay to want to stop it.

### Hand on the back
Even though it's often the upper back, it can still feel inappropriate. The lower back is almost always problematic if it's someone you're not involved with.

### Hand on the neck
When a Manchester City football striker placed a hand on the side of the neck of female ref Sian Massey-Ellis and pulled her towards him (17 October 2020), there was immediate recognition that this was an aggressive move. The charity Women's Aid lists 'holding you by the neck' as an act of physical violence. If it feels uncomfortable and you don't want it to happen, it's not okay for someone to do that to you.

### Hand anywhere near your breasts
Absolutely not okay. Nothing more to say really, unless you are convinced it was entirely accidental, like when a train slams to a halt and some poor guy is launched at you at 40 miles per hour.

## The Words

- Move out of reach. You can do this subtly by merely stepping back or as a more obvious motion with a large arch of the body away from the hand.
- A long stare at the hand before the above movement strengthens your message.
- If the toucher gets the message and apologises, say **Thank you** rather than "That's okay".
- **Remember, I'm not a touchy person** literally reminds the person that you don't like what they're doing.
- **I obviously need to wear a sign saying 'Don't touch me', don't I?** gets the message across that it's been going on for too long and you're not happy.

If it's been going on for some time and you want to be firmer:
- **I really don't like being touched. You must have forgotten.**
- **You obviously don't understand why, but I don't like to be touched.**
- **You need to stop touching me.**
- **I've asked you to stop touching me, and you have to respect that.**
- **You seem to be deliberately ignoring my request to stop touching me.**

If the toucher is male and only touches women, sound an alarm bell:
- **I've noticed you don't touch any of the guys this way.**
- **Ah, you didn't get the memo. I'm not a touchy-feely type.**

- **I come from a long line of non-touchers.**
- (Step back) **Personal boundaries. Thanks.**
- **This is making me very uncomfortable.**
- **Take your hands off me, now.**
- **What are you *doing*?**

## Hands On the Leg or Lower Part of the Body

This is where things become pretty black and white. Hand on the thigh, under the table? Not okay. Touching any part of your bum? Not okay. Everybody knows this, and it's usually done in a secretive way precisely because the offender knows too.

It's not that we're confused about whether it's inappropriate for many women, we just don't quite know how to respond. If you think back to any time it's been done to you, it's often in a situation where to speak up would mean to 'cause a fuss' or embarrass yourself. Anyone slapping you on the bum 'as a joke' is out of order too.

*In most situations, the 'funnier' a slap on the bum is,
the more mortifying it is for the woman.*

If you have to work with someone who's done this to you before, do whatever it takes to reduce your stress or fear and retain some feeling of dignity. Remember, though, it's never your *job* to prevent someone's appalling behaviour; that's on them.

## The Words

- If he's an under-the-table operator, keep your chair pushed out far enough so that it's visible to others.
- Wait till the person is seated then choose a chair not within touching distance. (This may take cunning on your part, as this type will often make sure he's the last to sit down.)
- Get up, if you need to. If you're embarrassed, excuse yourself to visit the loo.
- Be as direct as possible if it's a hand on the thigh or bum, not a fleeting touch.
- Look at the hand, then at the person; repeat until they remove the hand.
- Swat or brush it away or pick it up and place it on the table.
- Try not to laugh, even if you're shocked or dying of embarrassment.
- **Seriously?**
- **Excuse me?**
- **Your hand is on my leg.**
- **Hey – hands off, thanks.**
- **Remove your hand.**
- **Move away from me.**
- **Show some respect.**
- **When is this ever okay?**
- **What do you think you're doing?**
- **Did I say you could touch me?**
- **Move it or lose it.**
- **Do *not* do that.**
- **My body is not public property.**
- **You need permission to touch me (and I didn't give it).**

If you are angry enough to attempt public humiliation, that's fine, but we recommend reading the situation first. Don't put yourself in danger. Some men will react angrily to being publicly dressed down, even when they know they're in the wrong. We also don't recommend name-calling. Stick to the facts of a hand being somewhere it shouldn't be.

# Hugging

This depends on the context but is much more problematic in the workplace. We conducted an anecdotal Twitter poll in 2020 and found that most people agreed it was a context-based issue, although almost as many thought office hugging should be banned.

Some huggers feel they have a right to hug, ignoring repeated refusals; others genuinely believe that non-huggers really *need* a hug but have yet to see the light. We recommend a firm hand here, although we recognise it's a lot easier to deal with colleagues than a boss or relative. Again, COVID-19 has given us all a good enough reason to stay well away.

## The Words

- A non-verbal response when someone comes in for the hug is your best bet.
- As you approach the other person extend your hand for a handshake and plant your feet at least a foot away from them. (Unless you're very petite, it will be harder for them to pull you in if you're rooted to the spot.)
- Thankfully, our experience of COVID-19 allows you to wave from a few metres away. Make sure to start the waving before the other person gets anywhere close, so that you are understood.
- If they're coming in for a hug anyway, grab them by the hand and hold their forearm with your other hand. That creates a physical barrier as well as letting them know how you feel.
- If you end up in a hug after all that, send a message by keeping your hands by your sides and resisting the pull towards their body.
- To keep it inoffensive, try: **Don't take it personally; I just don't do hugs.**
- Another version: **I know you're not psychic, but I'm not a hugger.**
- **I prefer to shake hands.** Make sure not to sound as if you're asking permission. Make it sound like a done deal.
- Go for a handshake and say, **I'm a hand shaker, remember?**
- Put your hands up with a reminder, **No hugging required.**

## Shoulder or Back Massages

Some people think they have the magic touch and want to give everyone a stress-busting massage, while others don't even like massages in a spa setting. Writing in *Marie Claire* magazine, journalist Kaitlin Menza referred to shoulder rubs or massages as a "gateway touch".[3] While it can be an innocent stress-buster, it's also a fairly well-recognised tool, setting the scene for further touching if you go along with it.

*Trust your gut if it doesn't feel right.*

Given that a massage isn't a show of affection in the way a hug is, you can refuse without offending the other person quite as much. However, if you know it's being done as a way to invade your personal space and to touch you for longer than a few seconds, focus on protecting yourself rather than the other person – in other words, don't worry about offending.

## The Words

If you have a repeat massager who is heading in your direction, try:

- **Blimey, why does everyone think I like massages?**
- **Don't you come near me with those massaging fingers.**
- Or just a reminder: **I'm pretty sure I told you I hate massages. Thank you anyway.**
- **This is my idea of torture** should stop a lot of people in their tracks.
- **Nope, not doing a thing, sorry** also sends the message that it's not working.
- **I really, really don't like this** should signal your complete discomfort.
- **Can you make a note that I'm not into massages?** also tells him not to do it in future.

For a more serious tone, try:

- **This is bordering on inappropriate.**
- **That's enough, thank you.**
- **Okay, you need to stop this.**
- **This is making me extremely uncomfortable.**
- **I want you to stop.**
- **I'm only going to say this once: I don't want a massage.**

## Kissing (or attempting)

There are several types of kisses that can be problematic.

Kissing as a greeting is very tricky and depends on the context. If you work with someone but only see them occasionally, you might give a continental-style peck or two on the cheek as a greeting. But what happens if they're standing next to someone you don't know very well? What about the friend of a friend you're meeting for the first time who comes in for a kiss? Then there's the creep who kisses women at the first opportunity, or the kiss you're okay with which somehow ends up landing on your ear, or worse, your lips. What to do? It's a minefield.

As we mentioned, the dreaded air kiss or double kiss can result in some very embarrassing clashes, but they're often cultural and non-sexual. However, you don't have to accept anything that makes you feel uncomfortable. Anyone kissing you without your permission and in a sexual manner is not okay.

## The Words

If you're going to say anything, it's best to say it before the mouth is anywhere near your face, but it's often difficult to tell whether it's an incoming hug or a kiss. You have to anticipate both and act accordingly:

- **Probably not a good idea these days.** Who can argue with that?
- **Let's just stick to handshakes/elbow bumps. Better safe than sorry.**
- **Hi, I'm handshaking only at the moment.**
- **We're all probably a bit germ-phobic at the moment, so** — (offer hand or elbow).

A kiss that's sexual in nature and not welcome:
- See many of the *Words* for *Hands on the Leg*, above.
- **What are you doing?**
- **Don't ever do that again.**
- **That could land you in major trouble.**
- **Not sure why you thought that was okay, but it's not.**
- **I will not tell you again.**

## Non-verbal Attention

Often words aren't needed to make you feel uncomfortable, embarrassed or angry. Stares, sighs, whistles, leering, and blowing kisses and non-verbal communication can also be classed as harassment and is not to be dismissed if it offends you. It can also include someone touching himself in a sexual manner while in your presence, displaying sexually suggestive pictures and stalking.

One annoyance often reported in discussion threads is staring, while another is someone blatantly looking you up and down before starting a conversation or answering you. According to many reports, Netflix's harassment training for its film crews includes the advice that staring at someone for more than five seconds is creepy. Even if this is an urban myth, it's good to follow.

Invading your personal space (standing too close) can also be classed as harassment if it's not welcome. We've often had that experience where we keep stepping back, and the other person keeps advancing. Given that we all have different tolerances for this type of space invasion, start by assuming the invader is unaware of the offence unless you know otherwise.

## The Words

Staring:
- No words. Staring back without saying anything often makes the more timid starer look away.
- Placing something on a desk or between you to block the view might also work.
- Instead of immediately accusing, ask the person if there's a problem or if they need something from you. **Is there something I can help you with?** allows you to communicate that you can see the stares.
- Ask the person directly **What are you staring at?** or **Why are you staring at me?** If you get a denial, simply ignore it with **No, you were staring at me. Is there a reason?**

Space invaders:
- Keep an item in your hand to maintain a space between you. The Queen does this by holding a handbag in front of her body. Use your bag like Her Majesty or employ folders, clipboards, books, even a cup of coffee.
- Keep it light-hearted with, **Can you take a step back; you're so close you're out of focus.**
- Slightly more serious is **I have personal space needs, Bill** while taking a step back. Placing your hand(s) up with an outward-facing palm also tells him not to take a step towards you.
- With someone who is genuinely clueless, or who doesn't care, you may have to spell it out. **This is a little too up close and personal, Jamal.**
- A giant step back is often better than any words with a space

invader who is clearly trying to make you uncomfortable. If this isn't possible, keep it short and straightforward: **This is a little too close** with the outward-facing palm gesture. (Don't touch the invader.) Then quickly carry on with business.

- **One word – COVID** reminds the space invader of the need for distancing.

# Groping, Assault and / or Rape

## Grabbing and Groping

There is no grey area here. Sometimes it's done out of sight but in a very public place, and it relies on the fact that you probably won't 'make a scene'. The thigh grabbing under the table at a work or formal dinner, for example. Very often, this behaviour takes place where there are no witnesses. There's a reason for that – although the groper knows it's wrong and usually illegal, he doesn't care if you object or not, he only cares that there are no witnesses.

## Assault and rape

If you are assaulted or raped, this is a criminal matter. Experts acknowledge that not every victim wants to go to the police; only you can make that decision, but there are many support resources available, and we've listed several in the *Resources* section at the end of the book. If it happens at work, there may be support available. You can raise the issue at work as well as going to the police.

We recognise that assault or rape is a step above what we cover in this book. We also recognise that no matter how much 'training' women may go through to avoid and then cope with assault and rape, nothing is guaranteed. Not only does such training place the onus of prevention on women, how we respond in the moment is often not how we imagine we would. The UK government's Crown Prosecution Service states:

> *"Victims in a rape situation often become physically paralysed with terror or shock and are unable to move or fight."*

According to Rape Crisis (see *Resources* for contact info):

> *"The 'fight or flight' response is how people sometimes refer to*

*our body's automatic reactions to fear. There are actually 5 of these common responses, including 'freeze', 'flop' and 'friend', as well as 'fight' or 'flight'. The freeze, flop, friend, fight or flight reactions are immediate, automatic and instinctive responses to fear."*

Rape Crisis Scotland adds:

*"However, the truth is that nobody knows how they or anyone else will react ... it is very common for someone who is raped to respond quite differently to what we might expect. The way someone describes how they felt and what they did as an assault took place might surprise you and appear to be the opposite of what you thought. Many survivors describe freezing and feeling unable to move to escape, or to cry out or fight back, and this response is just as normal and natural as any other."*

Rape counsellors recognise that not all women want to report a rape, nor should they be forced or even persuaded to do so. This is even more important in a workplace situation since rape and assault victims worry about not being believed, about the incident being kept confidential, what will happen to them after they have come forward, the prospect of losing their job, workplace repercussions and many more valid concerns.

We encourage all rape and assault victims to talk to someone, but that person or organisation will depend on your unique circumstances.

# 5

# Sexists – How They React

As you may have already discovered, many people don't like it when you stand up to sexism. Sometimes the backlash is minor and not worth worrying about, and other times it can have serious consequences, such as risking your job or placing you in physical danger. At work, retaliation for speaking up about discrimination or harassment (also known as victimisation) is prohibited under the Equality Act of 2010, so again, keep notes of what's going on. Any retaliation against a colleague who helps you make a claim is also prohibited.

The worst retaliation seems to follow allegations of sexual assault or sexual harassment. As we've seen repeatedly in the press, the default is to question the woman's motives, blame her for what happened or defend the accused person.

You might also find that other women who have faced sexism don't support you. The thinking goes that they put up with it and so should you. Obviously, that doesn't mean it was acceptable, and ignoring ongoing behaviour usually means it will continue.

## Intersectionality

Many women experience sexism not just as women but also as members of other groups. Racialised sexual harassment combines sexism with racist slurs, stereotypes and threats. Research has found that women with disabilities have a more challenging time being heard. When it comes to reporting sexual offences, some people don't see these women as sexual beings and therefore don't believe their allegations. Women with psychosocial disabilities are often discredited due to their mental health history, and women with intellectual disabilities are doubted because of an assumed inability to tell the truth. Women with mental disabilities can also be seen as hyper-sexualised and lacking in self-control[1], in other words, having led the man astray or at least 'asked for it', while deaf and blind women can be seen as unreliable because of their limitations and generally need more corroboration to be believed.

It's crucial as a society we listen to all women and be aware of biases that may affect our perception, understanding or willingness to believe the sexism being reported.

## It's Not You, It's Them

When you speak up and stand up for yourself, and you're dismissed, it doesn't mean you don't have a point, it means the other person doesn't have empathy.

## What the Backlash Can Look Like

Created in 1997 by Dr Jennifer J Freyd, Professor of Psychology at the University of Oregon[2], this acronym helps us see what's really going on:

DARVO

**D**eny

**A**ttack

**R**everse the **V**ictim **O**rder

- When confronted with an accusation, people who do this will **Deny** the charge, telling you it didn't happen at all, that you imagined it or are exaggerating it.
- If this doesn't work for them, they go on the **Attack**, calling you names or accusing you of something.
- Many will **Reverse the Victim Order**, painting themselves as the injured party and you as the real baddie.

Dr Freyd's more recent research suggests that education (about DARVO) is crucial.

> *"We found exposure to the DARVO response was associated with less belief of the victim and more blame of the victim. In another experiment, Sarah Harsey and I examined whether learning about DARVO could mitigate its effects on individuals' perceptions of perpetrators and victims. DARVO-educated participants (compared with control) rated the perpetrator as less believable. While much more research is needed, these results suggest that DARVO is an effective strategy to discredit victims but that the power of the strategy can be mitigated by education."*

In other words, when people (including victims of sexism) are aware of DARVO and recognise it when it's happening, they are less likely to fall for it.

# Blaming #MeToo or Feminism

*"Feminist progress has been rapid and impressive in many ways. But this has led to resentment, anxiety and misogynistic backlash."*[3]

'Radical feminists' – this term is used for everything from women who supported Jane Austen on the bank note to more controversial policies that are still being widely debated. Often when people use it, it's to characterise as 'fringe' any kind of activity, action or statement to do with women's rights. Rather than encourage informed debate, users seek to shut it down.

Another contender is the #MeToo movement, which has "gone too far" so that men now "can't do anything". And by turning the phrase into a verb, men are 'MeToo'd' when we call them out on sexism. All are detractors, trying to belittle and marginalise not just the movement but the act of speaking out. Sadly, this is on the rise and is being worn like a badge of honour by some men.

A 2019 survey by LeanIn.Org and SurveyMonkey found that 60% of male managers say they're uncomfortable working with women, including mentoring, working one-on-one or socialising.[4] In extreme cases, the word on the street is not to hire women at all as it's 'too risky'. Ironically, men who vehemently claim they would never assault a female seem to be okay with accusing women of something extremely rare: falsely accusing them. And even more ironically, this backlash creates more, rather than less, of a Boys' Club and appears only to hurt women. As a 2018 Bloomberg business article noted though:

> *"… those men are going to back out of a sexual harassment complaint and right into a sex discrimination complaint."*[5]

In other words, if men try to avoid an unlikely sexual harassment claim by refusing to meet with women, they're very much at risk of discriminating against them by doing this.

## The Words

Although when blaming #MeToo or feminism comes up, the intent is to distract from your point, it's often very tempting to want to respond anyway.

"#MeToo / feminism has gone too far":
- **Until it's no longer a thing, it hasn't gone far enough or**
- **Look at the stats; we're not even close.**
- **Explain 'gone too far'.** (But bear in mind, you're inviting a debate.)
- **What was the final straw for you?** (Ditto.)
- **If you have a problem with #MeToo, you have a problem with people saying 'Yes, that happened to me too'.**
- **Are you not interested in stopping sexual violence?**
- **#MeToo was a response to women's experiences of sexual abuse and violence, so until that stops, no, it hasn't gone too far.**
- **The #MeToo movement isn't a plot to 'get' men. It's about women telling their stories to support each other and get rid of sexual violence.**

Blaming feminism:
- **The only thing it takes away is male privilege.**
- **Feminism focuses on women's rights without trying to remove others' rights.**
- Quote Maya Angelou: **Of course I am a feminist. I have been a female for a long time now. It'd be stupid not to be on my own side.**

**66**

*I myself have never been able to find out precisely what feminism is: I only know that people call me a feminist whenever I express sentiments that differentiate me from a doormat.*

Rebecca West,
British author and journalist

- **What's wrong with feminism? Surely you believe in equality and respect?**

If "toxic femininity" is mentioned, there are many options:

- **I think you have your terms confused. Femininity usually means passive, caring, compassionate and agreeable. How can that be toxic? The only toxic part is that we're all punished for not conforming.**
- **Toxic masculinity is when masculinity is taken to extremes and leads to harm, like rape and assault. What's the female equivalent of that?**
- **If femininity is compassionate, caring, passive, etc., then the only toxic version of that would be when we put others first to the detriment of ourselves.**
- **The only toxic femininity I know about is the one where we're forced to wear certain clothes, behave a certain way and accept less than men.**

"Men are losing their rights":

- **Tell me, what rights have you lost?**

"We can't do/say anything these days":

- **Damn right, because now there are consequences.**
- **That sounds like what you want to do/say is going to be offensive.**
- **Just because you got away with it, doesn't mean it was ever okay.**

## Deflection

Otherwise known as 'whataboutery', this is where people change the subject to avoid addressing your point or taking responsibility. Sometimes they point out a similar, previous incident: "What about last year when so and so did such and such?" Other examples include naming your faults (relevant or not), flinging so many accusations at you that you don't have time to respond and firing off so many complaints about you that your credibility is damaged.

When deflectors do this, they often manage to redirect the conversation, demanding that you address their points instead. Stay focussed.

"Not as bad as" is another form of deflection: "At least you're not in [names country] where women aren't even allowed out without a man/have to wear certain clothing/get married off young." Also known as 'relative privation', users seek to make your situation look acceptable when compared to a worst-case scenario. The other popular one is: "At least I didn't [names a far worse offence, from which you should be grateful to have escaped]." This is frequently used when women call out microaggressions.

## The Words

It's essential to keep your focus and not get sidetracked, which is the objective of whataboutery. In other words, don't take the bait.

In answer to "What about…?":
- **If that's a concern of yours, we can talk about that later. The issue now is…** or
- **I asked a question first.**
- **Nice try, now let's get back to the issue.**
- **The fact that you're bringing up something else tells me you can't answer my point.**
- **I see you're changing the subject.**
- **Tell me why that's relevant.**
- **That takes us off on a tangent, and it's not relevant here/we don't have the time at the moment.**

"Not as bad as" – pointing to a situation that's worse than yours as the example:
- **You're implying that your example is the only one worth bothering about, which isn't true.**
- **What you're talking about doesn't negate my problem.**
- **So you're saying that unless it's as bad as [name the example], no one should do anything about it? Not happening.**
- **It's one hundred per cent possible to care about both issues.** (Quite often, a way of shutting you up is to accuse you of not caring about other issues.)

At work:
- **If you're concerned about what so and so did, you should take it to HR. At the moment, we're talking about…**

## Dismissal

From the accusations that we're "too sensitive" to being told to "chill" or "get a sense of humour", we've all heard the various attempts to dismiss or negate what we say and our opinions. Other well-worn reactions include you're "playing the woman card" (not sure what other card there is to play, but see p.63), overreacting, virtue-signalling, being hysterical, shrill or the catch-all: a man-hater. From women you'll also hear "It didn't happen to me, and I'm a woman" and "You're fragile / a snowflake; get a backbone". The equivalent from men is that they have a wife / sister / daughter / mother who never complains about the issue.

## The Words

Sometimes it's not even worth replying to dismissive comments, but here are a few options if you need to:

"You're hysterical" etc.:
- **We're not talking about me at the moment, we're talking about you and what you said/did.**
- **There's nothing hysterical about wanting to focus on the issue.**

"You're getting emotional":
- **You sound like you're scared of human emotions.**
- **I have many emotions. This one happens to be frustration/irritation/annoyance.**
- **Yes, otherwise known as passionate about this subject.**
- **You seem to be getting angry; that's an emotion too.**
- **I care about this issue a lot.**

"You're getting defensive":
- **I have nothing to be defensive about.**
- **You're getting delusional.**
- **That's usually how people behave when someone's on the attack.**

"Calm down":
- **When has that ever worked?**
- **I am calm.**

**66**

*We need to reshape our own perception of how we view ourselves. We have to step up as women and take the lead.*

Beyonce, singer and actress

"No one else is complaining about him / this":

- **Of course not, he doesn't do it to everyone. That's how he gets away with it.**
- **That's not relevant.**
- **Have you asked anyone else?**

"I didn't mean anything":

- **Fine. I'm still asking you to stop.**
- **If you didn't mean anything, you wouldn't be arguing, you'd be apologising and trying to do better.**

"This happens to everyone":

- **No, statistics show it happens more frequently to women.**

"Strong women don't whine about this":

- **Pretty sure it takes strength to stand up for what you believe in.**
- **Oh, yes, because weak women definitely take this on.**
- **And even stronger women don't put up with it.**

## Gaslighting

The word comes from the 1938 play of the same name, in which a husband manipulates his wife into questioning what she knows to be true. Among other things, he dims the (gas) lights in the house while pretending that nothing has changed. Gaslighting is subtle and includes outright denials, lying, contradicting, blaming you, sowing seeds of doubt and manipulating the perception of reality, both to yourself and others. Phrases you'll hear include: *You're crazy; You have issues; You're a drama queen; I never said that; You're making false accusations; You're an attention-seeker.*

## The Words

When someone is disputing what you know to be true, arguing the point gives it oxygen, and since gaslighters have their own version of reality, it's often pointless. Dismiss it quickly and get back to the real issue. At work, if it's an ongoing situation, it's crucial to keep detailed records and create an e-mail trail if you can.

- **You and I both know that X happened/you said that/it's a problem, so let's get back to the issue.** Short of saying "We both know you're lying", this tells the gaslighter he's busted, and you won't let him derail the conversation.
- **Your recollection of what happened isn't correct.** If at work, add, **Here, my notes show the exact details.** This will not only help stop the gaslighting but also puts the person on notice that you're taking notes and taking control.
- In response to "I would never say that…", don't be put off. **You clearly would because you said it last Friday when we were talking about…** This lets the person know you're not to be conned.
- **Yelling at me doesn't change the facts.** (Gaslighters often respond aggressively.)
- Keep things on track with: **That doesn't change my point, which is…**
- Play innocent then keep talking: **I don't understand how your point fits in here, but…**

## Hitting On You

When women ignore or discourage men who are trying to chat them up or ask them out, they often receive a negative reaction. Most common is the chap who just won't give up, his preferred method being to wear you down or negotiate with you on how much information you'll give him. Right up there with it though, is the outrage or disbelief that you won't give them the attention they feel they deserve.

If they're annoyed or embarrassed, things can turn nasty quickly. Men's reactions can range from insults (isn't it interesting how a woman attractive enough to be chatted up suddenly becomes ugly and repulsive in a few seconds?) to physical gestures, actions, and even assault. Of course, the most important consideration is to make sure you are safe before responding.

## The Words

Avoid getting into a debate with these guys because they see it as a chink in the armour and a further opportunity to pursue you.

- **I'm not discussing this.**
- **I don't owe you any answers.**
- **Just because you're asking me all these questions, doesn't mean I have to answer.**
- **If you're offended, you only have yourself to blame.**
- **Please leave me alone or I'm walking away anyway.**
- **I don't want you to sit here.**
- **This isn't charming or romantic, by the way.**

## "I Was Only Joking"

This is a catch-all phrase for bullies trying to mock you or make you look ridiculous for objecting to what they say.

**"**

*All my life men like you have sneered at me, and all my life I've been knocking men like you into the dust.*

Brienne of Tarth, Game of Thrones

## The Words

- Okay, explain the joke.
- That's what bullies say.
- If that was your idea of a joke, you need new material.
- Do you always joke alone?
- You're doing it wrong then.
- Here's another one. When is a joke no longer a joke?
- And I was only not amused.
- That's disrespect disguised as a joke.
- No, you were rude.
- I think you know you've gone too far.
- Do you always make jokes at the expense of other people?
- I don't like jokes that try to make another person feel bad.
- That's the worst excuse in the world.
- Your joke backfired then.
- Do you see me laughing?
- Hmm, funny because it sounds like you meant it.
- It's possible to tell jokes without making fun of other people, you know.
- Let me be the adult here; I'll just ignore that.

If the person genuinely thought you would find something funny, a gentler approach is called for, but you can still point it out:
- I'm sure you meant no offence, but honestly, I find it rude / unfunny.
- I know you didn't understand. That's why I'm explaining it to you.
- You know, I just don't find that funny.
- I don't usually mind, but that went too far.

## "It Comes With The Territory"

Women who work in bars often hear this when they complain about being groped or harassed at work. Sadly, sometimes when you complain about sexism in a heavily male-dominated area, other women can also be dismissive, telling you that yes, it comes with the territory, you should be "strong" (and put up with it), and the old "in my day…" stories.

Again, bear in mind that if you're standing up to sexism where the testosterone is flowing, things might get nasty. Put yourself and your safety first.

## The Words

- Just because it's par for the course, doesn't mean it's not sexual harassment/assault and illegal.
- Me being here does not give you the right to do this.

To other women telling you they had to put up with it (and so should you):

- The fact that you're saying you had to 'put up with it' tells me you know it was wrong.
- Why would you wish someone else to go through what you did?
- I would have thought since you had to 'put up with it' you'd support anyone who was trying to stop it.
- What exactly is strong about saying nothing?

At work:

- If we just accept this as part of the job, even though we know it's wrong, it's never going to get better.

# Mansplaining

Using this word itself usually leads to a colourful assortment of reactions. Some people deny that mansplaining is a thing, that it's just condescending language, men do it to each other, women do it to men and so on. Some don't deny the mansplaining happened, they just don't think you should be complaining about it. They also miss the irony that while denying sexism in the form of mansplaining, they're more than happy to dictate what women should be thinking anyway. Others jump straight to the insults, which usually involve a claim of man-hating and, curiously, your marital status (single) and fondness for cats.

## The Words

Using the D (deny) in DARVO, men and some women simply claim "It's not a thing" if you mention mansplaining, which is partly why we recommend not using the word itself. If it slips out, try:

- **Millions of women say otherwise.**
- **Just because you don't want to hear it, doesn't make it untrue.**
- **Are you really mansplaining 'mansplaining' to me?**
- **You're now telling me (and other women) what my experience is.**

"Looking for something to be offended by" also comes under the D umbrella, by denying the existence of mansplaining.

- **We don't have to look for it; this stuff comes running.**

"Women do it to men too" shows a complete lack of understanding of the power structures at play:

- **Any kind of 'splaining' is done by the person with the most power. It's not women when they're talking to men.**
- **Oh, really, like how?** (If you have the stomach.)

"Men do it to each other too":

- **There's usually less/no power imbalance there, and they don't patronise each other as much as they do women.**
- **Perhaps, but that doesn't mean there's no mansplaining to women.**
- **Great. If they want to put up with it, fine. But I won't.**

**❝**

*My coach said I ran like a girl. I said if he could run a little faster, he could too.*

Mia Hamm, American soccer icon

"Man up and stop whining" is an example of the A (attack) in DARVO:

- **I'm pointing something out. Sorry you can't handle that.**
- **Whining is for wimps; it takes guts to stand up to this stuff, and I'm not backing down.**

"Don't you have bigger fish to fry?" accuses you of not caring about more serious issues:

- **I can walk and chew gum at the same time.**
- **So you caring about rape victims means you don't care about animal abuse then. See how that doesn't work?**

Accusing you of "womansplaining" is just making something up. It doesn't exist:

- **That would mean I'm telling you something you're already an expert in and clearly you aren't in this case.**
- **Have you noticed how that really hasn't taken off? It's not a thing.**
- **When women have the power in most situations, that might be a real thing.**

## "Not All Men"

A widespread response to sexism claims is to insist that you can't paint all men the same. While some men may genuinely not be 'that guy', interrupting you or derailing the conversation to tell you this is another attempt to dismiss your issue and put their agenda front and centre.

The point they're missing is that although of course we're not blaming 'all men' for everything, nearly *all* women experience the type of problems we talk about here, and that needs to be the focus. Additionally, while it's not 'all men', we're often surprised by who it turns out to be.

## The Words

- Not all men, but it happens to most women.
- It's not all men, but it's too many men.
- We know it's not all men, but it's not always easy to see who it will be.
- We know it's not all men, but if I gave you a tube of Smarties and told you four were poisoned, how would you react?
- Tell us how we're supposed to know who it might be.
- Just because you don't do it, doesn't mean that it's not happening and that most women don't experience it.
- It sounds like you're more concerned about the feelings of men who don't do it than the feelings of women who are experiencing it. Makes the point without phrasing it as a question.
- Being annoyed at what *some* men do is not the same as hating all men or blaming all of them.
- I know what most women go through might sound awful, but it happens. Instead of denying it, you could just listen.

However, you could take their point and run with it:
- That's excellent that you're not doing it. And perhaps add, So I'm clearly not talking about you.

## Questioning Your Motives

As we've seen with many headline-grabbing cases, one of the most common attempts to dismiss or negate an allegation is to question the woman's motives – especially if it's been a while since the incident. However, not reporting an offence immediately is very common, particularly with assault and abuse cases. There's even a hashtag for it: #WhyIDidntReport.

The fact that there are many reasons why women don't speak out at the time is lost amid the accusations of ulterior motives. The implication is that they must be 'after something', have a personal vendetta, that the event was invented or took place so long ago it no longer matters.

If it's happening at work, keep a record of incidents as they happen so that even if you don't immediately complain about them, you have documented that they were bothering you. If relevant, it's also evidence that you tried to address it.

## The Words

- At first, I just wanted to forget it, but it was wrong then, and it's still wrong.
- Often, there is little incentive for women to come forward; look what's happening now.
- Why did I wait? Oooh, I dunno. Perhaps I knew I would be treated like this.
- Why did I hesitate? Because it's my word against his, and you know who's usually believed?
- The fact that this didn't happen yesterday doesn't mean it didn't happen.
- I didn't address it immediately because I was too upset/scared at the time. Now that I've had a chance to think more calmly, I want to talk about it.
- I wanted to give him a chance not to do it again. He didn't stop, even when I said I was going to report him.
- I didn't think anyone would believe me/I didn't expect my complaint to be taken seriously.
- Because it's usually the person reporting these things that comes off worse.
- Because there's often a backlash – like this.

# Rejected Compliments

"You look great in that skirt."
"I just had to stop you to say you're beautiful."
"You don't look like a lawyer/mechanic/chef."

A common reaction from men who 'compliment' you is to expect appreciation or thanks. But presuming to pass judgement on a woman's appearance or judge them solely on how they look is not a thoughtful comment. It isn't about what they're doing, their taste or actions, it's all about how they appear to the speaker. And sometimes, when you show them you don't appreciate the comments, they can get nasty.

Women often report being stopped in the street to be told they're "beautiful", yet if they continue walking, the same man can become abusive and scary. Being told your sweater "really shows off your figure", for example, is a comment many women find inappropriate and might look annoyed about. This pushback often results in men telling them they should enjoy the attention or calling them ungrateful.

Remember: if the compliment is out of the blue and doesn't make you feel good, you don't owe them anything.

## The Words

"If someone said that to me, I'd be flattered" is a typical response when women push back at comments about appearance. What they'd do is irrelevant, and your options include:

- **Great, but I'm not** or
- **Yes, but I'm not you.**
- You could stick the knife in a little with, **Yes, but it depends on who the comment is coming from, doesn't it?**
- **Are you really telling me how I should think?**

The other common reaction is disbelief: "You're complaining about someone complimenting you?" You can reply to this in several ways:

- **I'm not complaining; I'm telling you I don't like it and want you to stop.**
- **I don't find it complimentary** or
- **It's not a compliment if it's not wanted.**

If you're 'reprimanded' for not thanking the person, your behaviour will be called into question. Sometimes saying nothing is our recommendation since these men can very quickly turn the whole thing around and make themselves the offended party. This is the RVO (Reverse the Victim Order) in DARVO. However, you can also remind them:

- **It was an unsolicited opinion, not a compliment.**
- **It's not a compliment, it's harassment.**
- **You're deliberately trying to embarrass me, but you think I should be grateful?**

**66**

*Don't change women to fit the world;*
*change the world to fit women.*

Gloria Steinem, feminist and author

Another RVO you might also hear is: "Wow, I can't say anything these days" – a ridiculous statement and best answered with an eye roll or a shake of the head. If you do want to reply, try:
- **Yeah, probably not.**
- **Well, if you're worried you might offend, not saying anything is the best approach.**

At work:
- **I can do my job without hearing comments on how I look, thanks.**
- **You interrupted my work to give me unsolicited feedback, and now you're annoyed that I'm trying to continue working?**
- **That's not what I want compliments about.**
- **If you like giving compliments, I'd love some on my work rather than my appearance.**
- **I'm pretty sure I needed my previous experience/ degree more than my dress sense to get this job.**

## Rejected Touching

Indicating to people that you don't like them touching you often makes them react out of embarrassment or feel you're too sensitive. Stand your ground. Whether you should be touched or not isn't their decision; they don't get to tell you what they are allowed to do to you.

If you think there is going to be a problem or an escalation of some sort, particularly at work, take notes: dates, locations, your words, their reaction.

## The Words

- Say what you like; I still don't want you touching me.
- It should be enough to know that I don't like to be touched.
- Your thoughts on my not being able to take a joke aren't the issue here.
- It isn't relevant that you don't understand – or agree with – why I don't like to be touched. The fact is, I don't.
- So you're saying your right to touch me trumps my right to tell you to stop?
- Why are you still touching me?
- I've asked you to stop touching me several times now. This is not funny.

At work:
- If the issue is discussed in your company's HR guidelines, point this out. **This is clearly in violation of company policy, you know.**
- Let the person know that you're prepared to take the matter further. **You're still touching me after I've asked you to stop. Shall we go to HR to discuss this?**

## Tone Policing

Sometimes when people can't find anything wrong with *what* you're saying, they'll criticise *how* you're saying it. Instead of picking your argument apart (because they can't), they adopt a moral or superior attitude and tell you to "watch your tone". Technically, tone policing falls into the microaggression category because it's often so subtle, you wonder if anyone else caught it. However, it's so regularly deployed, it deserves special mention.

A woman's tone can often be criticised for being too aggressive, too emotional, too angry, too arrogant (especially if we're armed with facts), too patronising (ditto) – the list is endless. Even when our voice is calm and measured, the 'tone' attack can still be used if what we're saying isn't to the listener's liking.

Tone policing is a deflection technique and demeaning, so one option is to ignore it and take the power out of it. (A massive eye roll might also be appropriate.) If you decide to challenge it though, remember it's intended to deflect. If you get sidetracked into a discussion of how you say what you're saying, the tone policing will have worked. Make your responses as brief as possible.

**The Words**

- What's wrong with my tone?
- How would you like me to have said it?
- My tone is factual and balanced.
- Let's not get distracted. I'm talking about X and Y.
- Sounds like you can't answer my question.
- I see you've run out of credible things to say.
- You might not like my tone, but that wasn't my question/intent.

## Victim Reversal

Unfortunately, one of the most common reactions when women allege anything – from microaggressions to rape – is to try to place some or all of the blame on them. Remember:

**DARVO**
**D**eny
**A**ttack
**R**everse the **V**ictim **O**rder

Victim reversal, or the R part of DARVO, reverses the situation, making the offender the victim and you the baddie. It demands that you think of his feelings, reputation, job, marriage, family or future. From politics to small business, the woman's experience is deemed less important than the harmful effect the accusation will have on the man, despite his possible guilt. This can come not just from the guy but from others, especially in a work situation.

Sometimes they point out what the woman *did* to 'deserve it': drinking too much, smiling or walking alone. Where you *were* when it happened can also be the 'fault': hotel rooms, dark roads, in someone's home alone; in the workplace, it can be having dinner alone with a colleague or client. And then, of course, there's *how* you were behaving. Too friendly (leading him on), too naïve or just not assertive enough? And what about your appearance ("What were you wearing?") or even your body type ("Can you blame me?")?

Some studies over the years backed up these sexist assumptions by concluding that slim, attractive women were partly to blame for their rapes because the men couldn't help themselves. Other studies have reported that overweight women must have somehow provoked their rape or consented because they are unattractive and therefore who would want to assault them.

On the positive side, a few studies have shown that keeping the language about victims of rape or sexual assault active rather than passive and focussing on the offender rather than the victim, has reduced the amount of victim blaming.[6]

Often when faced with your objection, the man in question will register hurt: "How can you say that about me?" Others might question your motives and suggest you're 'out to get' the guy, again painting him as the victim. Kate Manne, author of *Down Girl*, describes this as 'himpathy'.[7] She also points out that this ploy makes the issue all about the man and erases you, the real victim, from the picture entirely.

Men will also assert that you're trying to make them ashamed of being a man or you're out to 'get' all men. Again, making themselves out to be the victim.

The thing to remember here is that discrimination, harassment and abuse don't magically happen. They are committed by someone, usually willingly. If his job or reputation is so important, shouldn't he have thought about that before acting the way he did?

A close friend of Toni recently witnessed a classic bit of role reversal on a film shoot. A famous male actor was standing too close to the makeup artist, who firmly reminded him that she'd already asked him to respect her space. Instead of apologising or looking sheepish, he painted himself as the offended one by saying loudly enough for everyone to hear, "Rude."

## The Words

If faced with "How can you say that about me/him?":

- **How could you do this to *me*?**
- **No one forced you to say/do that. (Grow up and) stop making excuses for your faults.**
- **You need to take responsibility for what happened.**
- **Does it ever occur to you that *you* caused this?**
- **I'm recounting what happened last Tuesday.**
- **This isn't about how you feel; it's about what you did/said.**
- **Are you saying I shouldn't be talking about what you did?**
- **Not only did you say/do that, but now you're expecting me just to accept it and say nothing?**
- **If you hadn't done what you did, I wouldn't be saying anything.**
- To others: **I understand that this is shocking, but it doesn't change the fact that he did/said this.** (Keep the focus on the perpetrator and the voice in the active tense.)
- **I realise that it would be easier for everyone to believe him rather than me, but that is not the truth.**

Bringing the wife and family into it ("What about his family? He'll lose his job"):

- **He should have thought of that before he did what he did.**
- **You're asking me to consider that when he didn't.**
- **So we're going to ignore what he did and focus on my reaction?**

- *I'm* not ruining anything; I'm not the one who said/ did X.
- So what he said/did to me doesn't matter then?

Trying to lay some or all of the blame at your feet:
- So rather than telling Brian not to behave like that, you're expecting me to change my behaviour even though I did nothing wrong?
- If it was my fault, how come no one else did/said that to me?

In response to "asking for it":
- No one asks to be assaulted/raped/harassed/ bullied.

"You're ruining his reputation." The thing to remind others here is that no one forces offenders to do what they do:
- If his job is so important, shouldn't he have thought of that before acting the way he did?

Accusing you of "playing the victim":
- If you think I'm playing the victim then you're admitting there's a problem.
- I'm not playing anything. I'm speaking up for myself/telling it like it is.
- I *am* the victim (and I'm drawing attention to it).

Telling you you're rude or offensive:
- I don't have to be polite when I'm asking you not to do/say that to me.

"Guess I'm not allowed to say that anymore" deserves:
- It was never okay to say that.

- And yet, you said it anyway.
- Thank goodness.
- That works for me.
- Then why did you?

"OK, you win; I'm a terrible person" is pure manipulation, designed to make this person the victim:

- I'm talking about [name the problem] and not about your character.
- No one said that.
- Stop being so dramatic. We are talking about…

"He's innocent until proven guilty?":

- You're right, an accusation isn't proof, but neither is a denial.

"Men won't want to work with you." The implication being that you'll accuse all men of sexism or harassment:

- Surely, we all know how to behave even when no one is watching?
- So, he/they won't work with me because they can't trust themselves not to touch me?
- If a male is alone in a room with me, I'm statistically more likely to be touched inappropriately than he is to be wrongly accused.
- Your fear of being wrongly accused is you saying I'm going to lie about what happens.
- I don't go into meetings assuming Duleep is going to grope me so how is it okay to assume I'm going to lie about him?
- Have you any idea how insulting it is to have it implied I'm going to lie about a colleague?
- How is this going to work? I'm never going to be

allowed in meetings with males again?

- If you refuse to be alone with a female employee, you should do the same with male employees.
- I can't see how that's fair. I've never falsely accused anyone, and Marco has never been accused of groping anyone before, but you're going with the assumption that favours him?
- If male managers will only meet one-on-one with the guys, this is going to be very detrimental to women in this company.
- Women are always concerned about being alone with men in such situations. This is nothing new for us. How come employee concern is only now an issue? (Hopefully, the last four points will help your employer to see that this might not be legal!)

# 6

# Be An Upstander, Not A Bystander

*"Unless we all take action to intervene against sexual harassment, we remain part of the culture that enables it."*[1]

## Men, Listen Up

Welcome! Fighting sexism is something in which men can play an important part. Since you're reading this section, you want to support women. You have to be able to identify a problem before you can tackle it, and reading the entire book will give you much more insight into the issues and situations women experience. It will make your part in fighting sexism and supporting the women in your life that much easier and more valuable.

We know that many men want to be more supportive of women and aren't sure exactly how to do that. There are a lot of great books out there on the subject, although most are written by men. Here are some tips from the horse's mouth, so to speak:

Pay particular attention to 'microaggressions'. Although very obvious sexism is not as accepted as it has been in the past, it's being replaced by more subtle forms that some men (and some women) don't immediately recognise.

Listen to women. Just because you don't initially understand why a particular comment or gesture was offensive doesn't mean it wasn't intended or received that way. We appreciate it's baffling to some men, but this can include compliments; they might sound well-intentioned, but some can make us feel uncomfortable all the same. When we say we don't like them, that's all you need to know.

## Stand up to sexism every day

Standing up to sexism means:

- Doing so even when we're not there. If you only say something when there's a woman present, that effectively means you're okay with sexism.
- Telling guys to cut it out, and being serious. It's not a joke to us and if you're going to have our backs there's no room for 'mock' outrage.
- Speaking up as it's happening. Saying nothing in the moment and then mentioning quietly to us later that you thought some guy was out of order doesn't really help.
- Redirecting men back to the women they're ignoring, as in the real-life experience of Carol Smillie, mentioned in *Section 3*. Her husband recognised the sexism at play when she was looking at her dream car and refrained from answering the questions posed to him when they should have been directed at Carol, the person buying the car.
- At work, it means giving women a voice in meetings and gatherings, amplifying their points and encouraging other men to do the same.
- Refraining from insulting men by implying that they're a little bit feminine. No more "throwing like a girl/crying like a girl" or joking that guys are "on their period".
- In some cases, it could also mean ensuring that a woman is safe. Study after study cited in this book show that most women experience inappropriate comments, ranging from comments on their appearance to threats of physical assault. The added problem is the potential danger when women stand up to this stuff: many men see that as a threat to their manliness and become angry. We all know where that can

lead. Just as the original comments are unacceptable, so is turning a blind eye when you hear them.

If you're a guy who thinks he's doing everything he can to support gender equality, great, but we urge you to examine that belief. A survey by Promundo found:

> *"While most men say that they want to support gender equality, they are not necessarily taking steps to reduce gender discrimination, and harassment.... Real, sustainable change requires men to become full partners and allies in supporting gender equality and in ending discrimination and harassment. It also requires men to understand how various identities (such as race, gender identity, sexual orientation, religion, and ability) impact the equation."*[2]

## Doing your part at work

One of the best ways you can do your part at work is to tell us what you earn! It's fifty years since the Equal Pay Act, but a gender pay gap still exists and will take years to close. Although it's not the whole pay gap picture, when salaries are shrouded in mystery, it seriously hampers any woman trying to make a case for like-for-like remuneration. And it can be illegal.

According to the government's own website, Section 77 of the Equality Act 2010:

> *"... is designed to make unenforceable terms of employment, appointment or service that prevent or restrict people from disclosing or seeking to disclose their pay to others, or terms that seek to prevent people from asking colleagues about their pay, where the purpose of any disclosure is to find out whether there is a connection between any difference in pay and a protected characteristic. Any action taken against an employee*

> *by the employer as a result of conduct protected by this section*
> *is treated as victimisation within the meaning of section 27,*
> *as applied in the sections listed in the table in subsection (5)."*

That means for the purposes of finding out whether women are being unfairly underpaid we can ask and you can tell!

Standing up for women might not be a picnic though, since there's been a bit of a #MeToo backlash. A 2019 survey by LeanIn.Org and SurveyMonkey found that 60% of male managers were not comfortable participating in a work activity with women (a 32% rise from 2018), and senior-level men were twelve times more likely to hesitate about a one-to-one meeting with a woman, nine times less likely to travel together for work and six times more likely to reduce the number of work dinners.[3]

You'll hear some men saying they're never going to mentor or even meet with women again because, hey, you never know what guys can be accused of these days. We don't think much of that attitude and by ignoring or excluding women, they'll probably be staring at a discrimination claim before too long, because:

- If you refuse to meet with women on your own but continue to meet with men, that's called discrimination. It's literally treating one demographic differently based on their sex. So you're either not going to meet *anyone* in a one-to-one setting or you'll rethink that idea.
- You are doing the same to women that you're accusing us of doing. Your concern about being accused of something is based on the premise that women see all men as predators; in other words, we're lumping you all in the same category. (We don't, by the way. We just don't know who the predator is since some don't 'look the part'.) By implying that a woman could accuse you of something inappropriate, you're

lumping us all together in one potential accuser group. Just as men say #NotAllMen, women in this scenario could say #NotAllWomen.

- The chance of you being falsely accused is relatively small. Statistically, if a man and a woman are alone in a room, the woman is far more likely to come off worse. So while a man may be worried about the remote chance of a false accusation, statistically a woman has a far more realistic worry of something happening to her.

It won't always be easy to call out another guy for sexist behaviour, but equality will not happen without men. Let's do it together!

## White Women, Listen Up

In her book *Hood Feminism* Mikki Kendall reminds us that:

*"… an intersectional approach to feminism is key to improving relationships between communities of women, so that some measure of true solidarity can happen."*[4]

Just as we want men to call out sexism when they see it, women too should have each other's backs. Sexism at work is still a big problem, even if you have not personally experienced it, but intersectional discrimination is even worse. Women who fall into another protected category such as race, ethnicity, gender reassignment, religion, health, age or sexual orientation report not only facing overlapping forms of discrimination but receiving limited support from their white female colleagues.

White women must do the same things we ask men to do. We can't be silent when other women are on the receiving end of discrimination and harassment. If we are going to stand up to sexism, it can't be just sexism against white women.

## Older Women, Listen Up

Most of us recognise that just because we put up with something 'in our day' doesn't mean younger women should, nor does it mean they're whining if they object to it. Countless studies and reports show that while blatant sexism may be on the wane, discrimination and harassment are still rife. There is great strength in trying to stand up to this, and we encourage you to add your voice and support to younger women by listening to their experiences and helping however you can.

Older women are often more confident and assertive, or as Helen Mirren once said:

> *"At 70 years old, if I could give my younger self one piece of advice, it would be to use the words 'fuck off' much more frequently."*

Seasoned women need to remember that not all women feel self-assured, especially younger women who tend to be even less so while appearing confident and assertive. Pointing out how 'strong' you are and calling them spineless or snowflakes for objecting to something is incredibly counterproductive. These women need our support, not our sarcasm.

Helen McGinn, TV wine expert and author of The Knackered Mother's Wine Club, has worked in a fairly male-dominated industry all her life. She told us about her experiences and feelings about being supported:

> *"In terms of examples, I think I've been very fortunate because despite working in a (still) male-dominated industry, I've always been surrounded by strong, supportive women. My first boss was female and the wine team at Tesco was all-female for years. Having said that, I definitely had times when I'd walk into a room for a meeting as the (then quite young!) buyer for*

*the UK's biggest supermarket and I could see faces drop. I was once asked, in a room full of men, when my boss would be arriving. I had to explain 'she' wasn't and the meeting would be with just me.*

*"I dread to think how many aren't working in that environment, who don't have that kind of support."*

## Taking the Heat

Anyone standing up to sexism is likely to experience some backlash, and that includes men who support women. Interestingly, this backlash can come from men and women, for different reasons. Perhaps more obviously, many men believe the status quo works for them and they don't want to lose their piece of the pie (even if that's not how equality works). They react negatively or aggressively to upstanders, believing their own status or power to be threatened.

Women, on the other hand, sometimes question the motives of a male upstander, since he doesn't appear to have a stake in the issue. What exactly is he up to? There is also sometimes resentment that a man (who doesn't know what it's like to be a woman) is seeking to speak for us at all. Understandably, this puts many men off; as women discover every day, it's not easy to stand up to sexism but since you're still reading, you probably agree that it's simply the right thing to do. There's some good news too: according to authors W. Brad Johnson and David G. Smith, research shows that "when men call out gender inequalities, they are perceived to be more credible because they are not acting in self-interest".[5]

You might think your tiny little effort won't make a difference and therefore won't be missed, but as author and activist Laura Bates has said:

*"Just as the mosaic of Everyday Sexism is made up of tiny pinpricks, so too the solution can consist of joining the tiniest of dots."* [6]

## Reporting For Someone Else

Remember, under the Equality Act you can report discrimination you see happening to someone else at work. It gets better: this law also protects you from victimisation or retaliation that results from your action. Your employers are largely responsible for protecting employees from harassment under the Equality Act, so you're not only supporting the target of the harassment, you're helping your company deal with it and avoid liability.

## What To Say

This section's *Words* relate mainly to what men (and some women) can *say* to support women experiencing sexism. The consensus in bystander intervention training is to use the Four Ds: direct, distract, delegate and delay.

- Direct means confronting a behaviour directly either by talking to the offender or the victim: telling the offender something is not okay or asking the victim if she's okay.
- Distraction can be used when you're not comfortable with direct intervention or just want to redirect the focus of the people in the situation. It can also serve as a reminder that other people can see or hear what's going on, which might stop the behaviour.
- Delegation means enlisting someone else to help, again if you don't feel comfortable or able to do anything. If you see a situation in a club, for example, a burly bouncer might be better able to deal with it.
- Delay refers to after the fact, when you weren't able to do anything at the time. If immediate intervention wasn't possible or advisable, you might approach the victim after the event to offer help or support, or just to talk it over.

Sometimes it's slightly tricky, as stepping in and speaking for a woman can come across as controlling even if it's well meant.

It can make the woman look like she can't handle the situation and this, in turn, gives the offending person the chance to only listen to and respect men's voices. This is often termed the White Knight Syndrome. Try to read the room or, if it's appropriate, ask the woman if she wants you to intervene.

Men should know that many women will be just as fearful of a well-meaning stranger coming to the rescue as they still don't know you. For them, that could be an 'out of the frying pan, into the fire' situation. Discussion threads all over social media illustrate this fear yet many men focus on how offensive or upsetting it is for women to be suspicious. Please don't. Not only does this dismiss the women's experiences or valid fears, it centres your feelings in the discussion. This is particularly ironic when the discussion is about helping women.

Finally, before we come to the *Words*, it's essential as an upstander to remain silent and just listen. If a woman tells you that she's experienced sexism, don't try to explain that it wasn't intended that way, or worse, that it didn't happen; that's mansplaining. Validating someone's experience is a crucial first step in supporting that person, or as Gloria Steinem says:

> *"Women have to learn to talk as much as we listen. Men have to learn how to listen as much as they talk."*

**The Words**

*If you see something, say something.*

Although this section is generally directed at men and gives them options for supporting women, white women can use many of them too. As we have mentioned before, white women have benefitted more than other women from gains made in the past decades. We have a role in making true equality real.

### In general
Turn things around and ask the same question to the guy who's being sexist, especially if it's about 'juggling work and family' and other things that men have in common. You don't need to start a fight. Many men don't realise how sexist they're being, so telling them about your own realisation (when you said something sexist) helps explain without making them defensive. If you're having trouble convincing someone that his comments or behaviour aren't appropriate:

- **You don't know what she's put up with in the past and what is upsetting her.**

### What *not* to say
Although you might intend to help, sometimes it doesn't come out that way.

If a woman is trying to confide in you about an incident, don't bring your own experience of the offender into the discussion. Although you might be shocked at what you're hearing, remember that how someone behaves with you isn't always the full picture.

Words to AVOID include:
- **Are you sure that's what he said?**

- **Wow, that's not like James at all.**
- **I can't believe that.** (While you may intend just to register shock, it can come across as a refusal to believe what she's telling you.)
- **What did you say just before he did this?** (This implies that she might somehow have 'provoked' the situation.)
- **You need to be careful. You could ruin his reputation with this.** (Most women are fully aware that the consequences of speaking out can be negative for them and not the guy.)
- **Why didn't you say something?** Hopefully, if you've read the rest of this book, you'll know there are many reasons why women don't immediately speak up.

While empathy is all very well, what women don't need is to be sidelined while you recount your own experiences in an effort to be an ally.

- **I know just how you feel. Last week X said Y to me and I couldn't believe it.**
- **I had something similar last month, so you might want to try…**
- **Ah well, here's where you went wrong. I always say…**

You might think that teasing or insulting men couldn't possibly constitute sexism against women, but here's how that works. By likening men to women (which is rarely meant as a compliment), you're reinforcing the idea that we are somehow 'lesser'. Similarly, don't compliment women by telling us we're demonstrating stereotypical 'male' attributes.

- **Mike, you're catching like a girl.**
- **What a big girl's blouse.**
- **Is it that time of the month, Mike?**
- **Dawn, you sound just like one of the boys.**
- **You're not a bad X for a woman.**

## Banter/Jokes/Locker Room Talk

This includes someone defending what they're doing or saying by telling their target they were "only joking" and so on. Don't just ignore it because to women that looks like you're condoning it. It also encourages the offenders to keep on doing their thing.

Also, don't just call it out because there's a woman in the room. As authors W. Brad Johnson and David G. Smith say:

> *"When you confront another man, don't attribute your concern or offense to the fact that there's a woman in the room or that women might be offended… This implies that Bob's sexist comment would be acceptable if no women were in sight."*[7]

### The Words

- **It's not just banter and it could be against the law.**
- **Banter? You're on your own with that one.**
- **Calling it banter doesn't make it okay.**
- **Joking? No, you weren't.**
- **Hmm. What was the joke again? I missed it.**
- **That's just not funny.**
- **Isn't that what the school bullies used to say?**
- **Hey – cut it out.**
- **If it's no big deal, then you'll be okay apologising.**
- **Don't be a d\*\*\*.**

# Catcalling

Many men don't understand 'the fuss' about being catcalled, so we're here to tell you: it's embarrassing, humiliating, belittling and unwelcome to many women. It's also the scenario where most women experience the least amount of support, possibly because bystanders don't see it as particularly threatening or dangerous.

Catcalling is public harassment, pure and simple. Not only can it make women feel scared, anxious, depressed and otherwise not okay, it has practical implications too. We change our routes to everyday activities like work and exercise. Sometimes we avoid situations altogether. Even if we don't seem that bothered by it, you can help remove it by calling it out. It's already classed as harassment, and there's a move to make it illegal.

## The Words

- **Don't be a d\*\*\*.**
- **Not cool.**
- **Cut it out.**
- **That's enough.**
- **It's not harmless.**
- **You need to apologise for that.**
- **Are you *trying* to embarrass/humiliate her?**
- **Does your wife like it when you do that to other women?**
- **You know what you come across like when you do that?**
- Engage the woman in conversation and act like it didn't happen.

## Condescending Language

This can be difficult for guys to pick up on as it's very subtle. It's low-level sexism (also known as microaggressions) such as calling women "girls" and "love", and telling us to smile. These are often power moves by men, designed to make us feel small. In the workplace, it chips away at our confidence or professionalism.

If a woman complains about this, don't dismiss her by telling her it was meant as a joke or that she's seeing something that wasn't there. She isn't. She heard language designed to make her feel inferior. It's all in the context; words like "sweetheart", "love" or "darling" can often be the opposite of respectful.

## The Words

"Sweetheart/Love" — some men use these words out of habit, but it can still be dismissive and therefore not okay. Some women also don't take offence but bear in mind that we may say that because we're trained not to 'cause a fuss'.

- Repeat the sentence using her name or a non-belittling word instead of "girl".
- **Sid, saying 'Sweetheart' all the time looks as though you can't be bothered to remember her name.**
- **Do you need us all to wear name badges? You seem to be having a difficult time with names.**
- **Are you going to call me 'Sweetheart' as well?**
- **That's nice, darling.** (Call out their action by giving them a taste of their own medicine in a humorous way.)

If you know a guy means to be disrespectful:
- **Why are you talking to her like that?**
- **It would sound a lot more respectful if you used her name.**
- **Hey, she has a name.**
- **I'm pretty sure she doesn't want to be your sweetheart.**

If she's telling someone not to call her "love" and getting pushback:
- **Sam, just stop calling her 'love'. It's not hard.**

When you hear a guy reprimanding a woman for objecting:
- **She's not 'taking it the wrong way'. You're saying the wrong words.**
- **She's telling you she doesn't like it. That should be enough.**

## Dismissal

Men (and some women) often dismiss women's opinions, concerns, experiences and objections. This can be done in various ways (discussed previously), and there's often a backlash when we stand up to it. This backlash usually attempts to gaslight women into thinking we're making 'something out of nothing', claims we don't have a sense of humour or resorts to insults to shut us up. There are a lot of actions other people can take to support women in these situations.

## The Words

When men laugh at women who are offended or embarrassed and try to tell them "it's nothing":
- **Just because it hasn't happened to you or someone you know, doesn't mean it's not real.**
- **You're trying to dictate how she should feel.**
- **Why don't you just listen to what she's saying?**
- **Do you always laugh at people after you've offended them?**

Saying "my wife doesn't mind":
- **Women don't have one collective brain. They don't all think and act the same as your wife.**
- **Have you even asked her?**
- **You *think* she doesn't mind.**
- **What relevance does that have here?**

Telling women there are bigger problems to worry about (e.g. focus on rape instead of standing up to microaggressions):
- **It's not an either-or situation.**
- **That's like you saying 'Save the elephants' and I say 'You don't care about tigers'. It doesn't work like that.**
- **It's actually possible to think about more than one thing at the same time, John.**

Suggesting we're "looking to be offended":
- **She doesn't have to look very far then. That was offensive.**
- **Why would she do that?**

## Getting Physical

This area is fraught for women because it involves physical strength, which adds an extra layer of danger and fear. It's also the least likely to be witnessed by others, which makes it hard to be an upstander in the moment. Often it becomes our word against the man's. If he's known as a 'decent' guy, the woman then comes under attack. However, if it's going on, it's everyone's responsibility to put an end to it.

## The Words

- Rohan, it's pretty clear she doesn't want you doing that.
- You don't need to know why. Just that she doesn't want you doing that.
- Jack, you have no idea why she might not want you to touch her, but she doesn't, and that's that.
- She's not too sensitive/making a fuss. She just doesn't want you to do that.
- It's not about what you want, it's about what she wants. And that's to be left alone.
- You need to remember the two-metre rule, and then double it.
- Take your hands off her.
- Pat, just because you've had a lot to drink doesn't mean it didn't happen.

At work:

- **I'm taking notes, by the way.** (This hints that a complaint could go further and you'd be a witness.)
- **You must have missed the memo saying 'no groping in the office'.**
- **Do we need to go down to HR to discuss this? I'm happy to help clarify the rules for you.**

## Hitting On Her

It can be difficult for men to know what to do when a guy is hitting on a woman and it looks like she's not okay with it. For a start, if you don't know her, how is she to know you're any better than the creep she's trying to get rid of? This is quite a common fear when women are 'rescued', and many men take personal offence. Please don't. It's not about you – and that's exactly the point. These women don't know you; they don't know that you're a good guy. But just as importantly, they don't know if you're not.

## The Words

If he's your friend:
- **Come on, Leo. She's said 'No Thanks'.**
- **You don't need to know why. Just that she doesn't want you bothering her.**
- **You're not helping your case by insisting.**
- **She doesn't owe you anything. Leave her alone.**

If you don't know her or the guy, instead of inserting yourself into the situation (and possibly making her even more worried), try:

- **Excuse me** (to the guy), then to her: **Hey there, let me know when you want to get that taxi. I'm over in the corner.** Don't stick around, but this will suggest to the guy you're a friend or colleague and she's not on her own. She can also come over if she really needs to get away, just don't expect too much, as discussed earlier.
- Take a drink over (but don't be offended if she doesn't actually drink it): **Hey, you left this over there. We're over in the corner by the way.**
- Try mouthing **Are you okay?** to her, but intervening with that question might anger the other guy. The aim here is to end the situation, not start a fight.

## Insults

Insults are often used when someone is out of ideas but full of anger anyway. Men who compliment women and don't get thanked resort to it, as do men who get turned down for a date, and men who 'don't believe' in feminism or show other forms of sexism. Even if you're in a 'sweary' environment, there's a difference between general swearing and words used to insult women. However, too much swearing at work can create an environment that meets the Equality Act definition for harassment.

A word for women: while we're not saying all female bosses are nice people, using gendered slurs such as "bitch" only serves to reinforce stereotypes that also work against you.

## The Words

"Bitch" – the response to being called out for using the B-word is that "women call each other bitch too". However, you don't need us to tell you that it's usually derogatory when coming from a guy.

- **Hey, that is *not* okay.**
- **Seriously? Cut it out.**
- **That's enough.**
- **She's doing the same thing that John did yesterday, and you never said a word to him?**
- **How come you lay into women who do this but not the guys?**
- **So you're just going to terrorise her into liking you?**
- **Do you talk to your daughters/sisters like that?**
- **Do you talk to your male colleagues like this?**
- **Are you seriously arguing against equality?**

"Frigid" – usually what we're called if we don't register interest.

- **Is a woman who's not interested in you automatically frigid?**
- **She obviously has more taste.**
- **You need a dictionary. She just doesn't fancy you.**

## Interruptions

Many men don't even notice interruptions because it doesn't happen to them very often. It can be hard to take a stand about something you're barely aware of, so the first step here is to take stock of the situation. How many women are present? Are they being allowed air time? If you notice a woman being constantly interrupted, or a guy who interrupts every woman, step up.

## The Words

- If you let her finish, she'll probably get to that.
- Keep going, Jane.
- Interrupt the interrupter. I'd like to hear the rest of Sabrena's point.
- Do you know how often you interrupt?
- Amplify her voice: That's an excellent point. Say it again, Izzy, I didn't hear the end of it.

At work:
- Shouldn't Tamara be talking about this?
- Let's bring Anna in on this one.
- Can we let everyone finish their thoughts before we jump in?
- Let's go back to Pilar's comment before we lose it.
- Let's keep the questions until we've heard everything, otherwise we're wasting time.
- Let's pick up on what Ali said because that was a really good point.

## Mansplaining

If there's one area men need to read up on, it's mansplaining, since we find a lot of men don't recognise it when it's happening.

Mansplainers come in two flavours – those who don't even realise they're mansplaining and those who know and don't care. Of the second group, some men don't care that they're mansplaining even though they know they haven't a clue about the subject.

## The Words

Help hand the mic back to the woman:
- **Josh, I think Kaya's got this.**
- **Alex, really?**
- **Pete, you should probably stop talking and let Kim handle this.**

At work, remind the room of her qualifications/expertise:
- **Don't know about anyone else but I have complete confidence in Talia on this one.**
- **I'd rather listen to the expert if that's okay.**
- **Aisha's here because she's the expert on this.**

Interrupt the mansplainer and stop him in his tracks:
- **How exactly would that work?**
- **Where did you get your degree in X?**
- **When have you worked on this?**
- **Okay, now you're just embarrassing yourself.**

## Unwanted Comments

If you haven't noticed, men comment about women all the time. Clothing, body, face, habits, competence, mothering, not-mothering, age – the list goes on. These comments are often irritating because we aren't looking for feedback; even what looks like a compliment can chafe if we don't care what that person thinks. Very often, though, the comments are belittling, embarrassing or downright hurtful and are intended to be so.

When women object to unwanted comments, we're told to "relax", be grateful for the attention or get ourselves a sense of humour. Often, our objections ramp up the disrespect for us, making it more difficult to speak up in the future. You can help here.

## The Words

- **It's not a compliment when it makes her feel awful.**
- **Hey, that's not okay.**
- **Paolo, why do you think she's interested in your opinion?**
- **I don't think she cares what you think.**
- **Okay, now should we critique *your* looks?**
- **She doesn't need to relax; you need to cut it out.**
- **Ollie, just imagine someone saying that to your wife/daughter.** (It would be nice if men didn't need this intervention to see how inappropriate they are, but hey, with some, it's the only way.)

If the excuse is "I was joking":
- **Hmm, isn't that what bullies say?**
- **OK, let us know when you get to the punch line.**
- **Do you see her laughing?**
- **No, you weren't.**

At work, there is never a need for comments on a woman's appearance/outfit/body, and even if you can't see the inappropriateness, if the woman needs support, step up. Better still, shut it down even when there are no women around:
- **Zack, why don't you stick to talking about work?**
- **She doesn't need to hear your opinion on her looks, Ed. She's here to work.**
- **Pretty sure she got this job on her merits, pal.**
- **Do you honestly think that's gonna work?**

# Resources

**Citizens Advice** – www.citizensadvice.org.uk
Links to England, Scotland, NI and Wales pages. Advice on discrimination.

**Rape Crisis** (England & Wales) – https://rapecrisis.org.uk
**Rape Crisis** (Northern Ireland) – https://rapecrisisni.org.uk
**Rape Crisis** (Scotland) – http://rapecrisisscotland.org.uk
A feminist organisation that supports the work of Rape Crisis Centres across England, Scotland and Wales. Also raises awareness and understanding of sexual violence and abuse in all its forms. Contains links to many other resources. Its national Freephone helpline is 0808 802 9999.

**Rights of Women** – https://rightsofwomen.org.uk
Free and confidential legal advice for women in England & Wales experiencing sexual harassment. Call 020 7490 0152.

**Victim Support** (for England & Wales) – www.victimsupport.org.uk Helpline: 0808 168 9111 (24-hour support). There is also an online chat option.

**Victim Focus** – www.victimfocus.org.uk offers a free e-learning course, 'Caring for Yourself after Sexual Violence' on the website.

**The Women's Equality Party** site contains a comprehensive list of support available to women:
www.womensequality.org.uk/support.

## Resources for Work-related Issues

**Acas** Guidelines on dealing with workplace sexual assault issues – www.acas.org.uk/sexual-harassment/handling-a-sexual-harassment-complaint Helpline: 0300 123 1100

**Citizens Advice** – www.citizensadvice.org.uk Links to England, Scotland, NI and Wales pages. Advice on discrimination.

**Equality, Advisory & Support Service** (EASS) – www.equalityadvisoryservice.com
Advises and assists individuals on issues relating to equality and human rights across England, Scotland and Wales. Open Monday to Friday 9am to 7pm and Saturday 10am to 2pm. Freephone Telephone 0808 800 0082. There is also an online support option.

**Protection from Sexual Harassment** booklet – Explaining the law and your rights. Published by the TUC. May 2019. ISBN 978 1 911288 49 7

**Scotland Employment Tribunal Customer Care** – 0300 790 6234
www.gov.uk/courts-tribunals/employment-tribunal

If you become the victim of a backlash because you have complained about someone at work, these websites can also help with that.

# References

### Introduction

1.  Victoria Waldersee (2018). #MeToo has made us more open to talking about sexual harassment, say majority of Britons. YouGov research conducted 2016, reported 2018: https://yougov.co.uk/topics/politics/articles-reports/2018/11/02/metoo-has-made-us-more-open-talking-about-sexual-h

2.  Purna Sen (2019). What will it Take? Promoting cultural change to end sexual harassment. *UN Women*.

### 1. Give Yourself A Talking To

1.  Robyn K. Mallett & Kala J. Melchiori (2014). Goal Preference Shapes Confrontations of Sexism. *Personality and Social Psychology Bulletin, 40*(5), 646–656 © 2014 by the Society for Personality and Social Psychology, Inc.

2.  J. Dahl & T. Vescio (2013). Sugar-coated Discrimination: How Subtle Sexism Undermines Women. *Harvard Business School*.

### 3. Sexists – What They Say

1.  N. Bostock (2019). BMA promises 'urgent investigation' into sexist treatment of top women GPs. GPOnline, 1 April 2019.

2.  Plan International (2020). plan-uk.org, 20 August 2020.

3.  N. Bodoky (2018). Complimenting Women At Work Is Sexual Harassment. SHESAID.com, 23 July 2018

4.  More Than My Height:
    https://amallitalli.com/blogs/tall-fashion

5.  Don Zimmerman (1975). Sex, Roles Interruptions
    & Silences in Conversation. *Current Issues in Linguistic
    Theory*, doi:10.1075/cilt.125; A. Hancock and B. Rubin
    (2015). Influence of Communication Partner's Gender
    on Language. *Journal of Language & Social Psychology*,
    *34*(1)

6.  K. Snyder (2014). How to Get Ahead as a Woman in
    Tech: Interrupt Men. *Slate Magazine*, 23 July 2014:
    https://slate.com/human-interest/2014/07/study-
    men-interrupt-women-more-in-tech-workplaces-but-
    high-ranking-women-learn-to-interrupt.html

7.  R. Solnit (2012). Men Still Explain Things to Me. The
    Nation:
    www.thenation.com/article/archive/men-still-explain-
    things-me/

8.  Laura Bates (2016). Mansplaining: how not to talk to
    female Nasa astronauts. *The Guardian*, 13 September
    2016

9.  B. Brogaard (2019). The 3 Most Subtle but Insidious
    Kinds of Passive Aggression. *Psychology Today*, 22
    October 2019

10. Paul A. Gigot (2020). The Biden Team Strikes Back. *Wall
    Street Journal Opinion*, 13 December 2020

11. L. Bian, S-J Lesley & A Cimpian (2017). Gender stereotypes about intellectual ability emerge early and influence children's interests. *Science, 355*(6323), 389–391

12. Natasha Quadlin (2018). The Mark of a Woman's Record: Gender and Academic Performance in Hiring. *American Sociological Review, 83*(2), 331–360. Article first published online: 15 March 2018; issue published: 1 April 2018

## 4. Sexists – What They Do

1. The Crown Prosecution Service: https://www.cps.gov.uk/legal-guidance/rape-and-sexual-offences-chapter-7-key-legislation-and-offences

2. Heather Flowe & John Maltby (2017). An experimental examination of alcohol consumption, alcohol expectancy, and self-blame on willingness to report a hypothetical rape. *Aggressive Behaviour,* doi: 10.1002/ab.21745

3. K. Menza (2017). Beware the Shoulder Rub: It's a Gateway Touch – and it's Distressingly Common. *Marie Claire*, 9 October 2017

## 5. Sexists – How They React

1. S. Ortoleva & H. Lewis (2012). Forgotten Sisters - A Report on Violence Against Women with Disabilities: An Overview of its Nature, Scope, Causes and Consequences. Northeastern University School of Law Research Paper No. 104–2012, 21 August 2012

2. J.J. Freyd (1997). Violations of power, adaptive blindness, and betrayal trauma theory. *Feminism & Psychology, 7*(1), 22–32

3. K. Manne (2017). *Down Girl: The Logic of Misogyny.* Penguin Books.

4. 2019 Survey conducted by LeanIn.Org and SurveyMonkey: www.surveymonkey.com/newsroom/men-continue-to-pull-back-in-wake-of-metoo

5. G. Tan & K. Porzencanski (2018). Wall Street Rule for the #MeToo Era: Avoid Women at All Cost. *Bloomberg Business,* 3 December 2018

6. L. Niemi & L. Young (2016). When and Why We See Victims as Responsible: The Impact of Ideology on Attitudes Toward Victims. *Personality and Social Psychology Bulletin, 42*(9), 1227–42; G Bohner (2001). Writing about rape: Use of the passive voice and other distancing text features as an expression of perceived responsibility of the victim. *British Journal of Social Psychology,* 40, 2001, 515–529

7. K. Manne (2017). *Down Girl: The Logic of Misogyny.* Penguin Books.

## 6. Be An Upstander, Not A Bystander

1. Elizabeth Broderick, Founder of Male Champions of Change: https://championsofchangecoalition.org

2. Promundo-US (2019). So, You Want to be a Male Ally for Gender Equality? (And You Should): Results from a National Survey, and a Few Things You Should Know. Washington, DC: Promundo

3. 2019 Survey conducted by LeanIn.Org and SurveyMonkey: www.surveymonkey.com/newsroom/men-continue-to-pull-back-in-wake-of-metoo

4. Mikki Kendall (2021). *Hood Feminism: Notes from the Women White Feminists Forgot.* Bloomsbury Publishing.

5. W.B. Johnson & D.G. Smith (2020). *Good Guys: How Men Can be Better Allies for Women in the Workplace.* Harvard Business Review Press.

6. Laura Bates (2014). The men who help fight back against everyday sexism. *The Guardian*, 14 March 2014

7. W.B. Johnson & D.G. Smith (2020). *Good Guys: How Men Can be Better Allies for Women in the Workplace.* Harvard Business Review Press.

# About the Authors

Toni Summers Hargis is an author and columnist. With a law degree and a Masters in Organisation Development under her belt, she spent years working in corporate HR, Training and Organisation Consulting. Always ardent and vocal about women's rights and equality, Toni was termed "difficult" in many a meeting and strives to continue in that vein, calling out sexist BS at every turn. She has written about women's rights issues for the past several years at Huffington Post, Medium and the BritMums website. Catch up with her on Twitter @ToniHargis and at tonisummershargis.co.uk.

BritMums is the UK's original influencer network, leading the online conversation since 2008. When Toni approached co-founders Jennifer Howze and Susanna Scott with the idea for this book, it fitted perfectly with the BritMums ethos to empower women and promote their voices and insights. Jennifer is an award-winning former *Times* journalist and an active supporter of women's rights through her political and editorial work. Susanna is a former Silicon Valley marketer recognised as a digital pioneer in the UK for championing the power of individual women's influence. @britmums

Printed in Great Britain
by Amazon